Institute of Commonwealth Studies
Ox

GUYANA

A Composite Monograph

Brian Irving, *Editor*

Published by:

INTER AMERICAN UNIVERSITY PRESS
Hato Rey, Puerto Rico 00919

For information write   Inter American University Press
                                     Box 1293
                                     Hato Rey, Puerto Rico 00919

Manufactured in the United States of America
Library of Congress Catalog Card Number #72-91600
International Standard Book Number #0-913480-05-3

Current printing (last number):   10   9   8   7   6   5   4   3   2   1

CONTENTS

There runs a dream of perished Dutch plantations
In these Guiana rivers to the sea.
Black waters rustling through vegetation
That towers and tangles banks, run silently
Over lost stellings where the craft once rode
Easy before trim dwellings in the sun
And fields of indigo would float out broad
To lose the eye right on the horizon.
These rivers know that strong and quiet men
Drove back a jungle, gave Guiana root
Against the shock of circumstance, and then
History moved down river, leaving free
The forest to creep back, foot by quiet foot
And overhang black waters to the sea.

      There Runs a Dream
      by A.J. Seymour

INTRODUCTION

Introduction

In 1964, the Caribbean Institute and Study Center for Latin America of Inter American University published the results of its first conference on British Guiana. At that time, two years before independence, distinguished leaders from Guiana were invited to attend sessions held at San German, Puerto Rico. Six years later that earlier study has been followed up to determine what progress has been made during those momentous years that witnessed the independence of Guyana and her efforts to solve those problems common to all of the newly emerging nations.

Guyana possesses a special interest for Inter American University. Over the years a large number of Guyanese students have studied at Inter American University and have returned to Guyana where many of them are now in positions of leadership. Moreover, Guyana has not been the subject of much scholarly research and we therefore hope that what light we may shed on the problem of Guyana will serve not only to enlighten those outside Guyana, but will also be useful to the Guyanese themselves as an objective attempt to clarify problems which presently exist in that nation.

The central problem which emerges from our study is the problem of creating unity in a land of diversity. Guyana, like many of the newly independent nations of the globe, is an artificial creation from a geographic standpoint. The problem of boundaries had led to disputes with Venezuela and Surinam both of which claim large areas of Guyanese territory. Added to the geographical problems is its ethnic diversity. Guyana's population includes Indians, Portuguese, Amerindians, Europeans, Chinese, and a large number of mixed racial strains. Diversity is also evident in the religious sphere, which includes Roman Catholics, Hindus, Protestants, Moslems, and tribal religions in the interior.

Another element of disunity is the lack of agreement among leaders of the country as to the political and economic means best suited to solve problems of the present and future. There are those who advocate communism as the proper course for the country to pursue. Others believe that private enterprise and a parliamentary democracy is best for Guyana. Still others favor a mixed form of socialism and private enterprise and some sort of "guided" democracy.

Critics of Guyana and her leaders must take into account the enormous problems confronting her. It may be that for the present Guyana's problems are insoluble and that long years of civil strife and economic chaos are necessary before she can begin to surmount those obstacles which bar her progress. More optimistically, however, Guyana has already surmounted problems that once appeared to be incapable of solution. The reason is that above all there had been at critical moments a tendency to work together to solve common problems. It is the fundamental good sense of the Guyanese people that engenders a feeling of optimism for the future.

Brian Irving

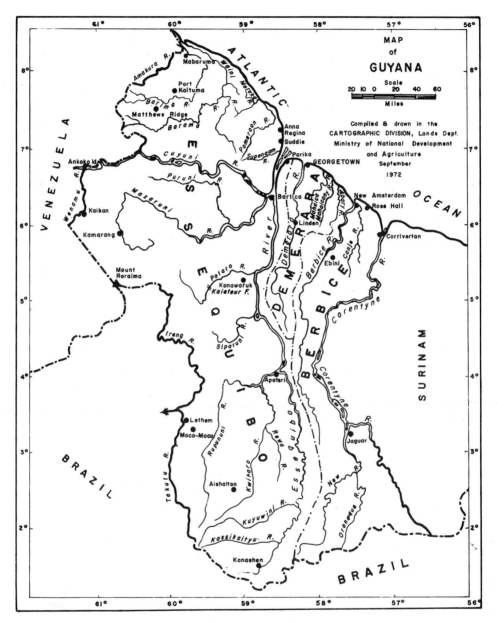

MAP courtesy of Ministry of National Development and Agriculture Cartographic Division, Land Department Law Courts, Georgetown, Guyana.

GUYANA

A BRIEF HISTORY

Brian Irving

Guyana lies on the north coast of South America, sandwiched between Venezuela on the west, Surinam on the east and Brazil on the south. Its Atlantic coastline of 270 miles ends at the Courantyne River which flows to the Brazilian border to a depth of 400 miles. With a territory of 83,500 square miles, Guyana is approximately the size of Britain but has a population of only 728,000.

Guyana is rich in resources: a carpet of fertile soil, two rainy seasons and plenty of sunlight throughout the year permit, in many cases, two annual crops on the coastlands. Vast tropical hardwood forests, interspersed with savannahs suitable for cattle grazing, cover its hinterland. A variety of minerals including bauxite, gold, diamonds, columbite, tantalite, iron and manganese are found here. Its many rivers provide natural communication between the coast and the interior and offer possibilities for cheap hydro-electric power.

The present population of Guyana consists of 352,000 East Indians, 212,000 Africans, 84,000 of mixed origin, 44,000 Chinese, 32,180 Amerindians, 6,200 Portuguese and 1,200 other Europeans.

The pre-Columbian inhabitants of Guyana were the Arawaks and Caribs who were either exterminated or driven into the hinterland. In 1498 Columbus, sailing along the coast, was unable to land because of inhospitable mudbanks and unhealthy marshes. In 1549 a band of Spaniards returned to the territory but soon retreated.

English interest led Sir Robert Dudley to investigate the rumors of an Empire of Guiana in 1594. Almost immediately Sir Walter Raleigh, lured by the legends of El Dorado, sent an expedition to the mouth of the Orinoco and penetrated 400 miles inland. Several other

5

English expeditions subsequently visited Guiana but did not establish any permanent settlements.

In 1598 the Dutch made their first voyage of inspection to Guiana. The Dutch reports frequently mentioned meetings with small English vessels along the rivers, and suggest that the English made trading voyages among the Guiana Indians who were very friendly to them. The English under Captain Charles Leigh in 1604, and again in 1609 under Robert Harcourt, attempted to set up small colonies but were very unsuccessful.

The next Guiana expedition of importance was Raleigh's last voyage of 1617. Raleigh had been released from the Tower by the King in order to make that last voyage. The King was interested in the gold mines Raleigh had promised to unearth. The expedition was thwarted by the Spaniards, and Raleigh returned to England and his own execution.

In 1612 the Dutch West India Company was formed in an attempt to regulate and organize contraband trading in Spanish waters. The Company was authorized to plant colonies and was given the right to take slaves from Africa in order to supply cheap labor for its future American possessions.

The Company drew up a scheme by which it would give feudal rights to "patroons" who would buy coastal and riverbasin areas and settle up to fifty people on them; the patroon received rent and exercised sovereignty in matters of law and policy. In 1672 the first patroon, Abraham van Pere, settled on the Berbice at his own expense. Van Pere was also connected with the first project to grow sugar in 1837, but the cane was actually grown in the Essequibo colony, location of the Dutch fort of Kijk-over-al, or "Look over all" the seat of Dutch government in the area. In 1637 the Dutch were well enough entrenched to send an expedition to the Orinoco to sack the Spanish settlement of San Thomé. By 1662 the colony was thriving, but its prosperity was short-lived; a force sent from Barbados by Lord Willoughby attacked the Dutch settlements and conquered Kijk-over-al. It was a major setback for the colony and the planters moved east to the new Dutch colony of Dutch Guiana, "Surinam."

The Dutch did return and by 1704 their plantations and farms were spreading along the riverbanks and the colony had regained its prosperity. Three decades later, however, Dutch trade in cotton, dyes, wood, spices and indigo with the Amerindians was waning and the more profitable business of sugar cultivation was accelerated. In 1738 Laurens Storm Van's Gravesande, secretary to the Dutch Governor, began a systematic development of the area. Gravesande became Governor in 1742, and during his tenure the colony grew rapidly. In 1775, the year of Gravesande's death, the colony included 300 plantations employing some 10,000 African slaves.

In 1781 war broke out between England and Holland. Demerara, Essequibo and Berbice settlements were conquered by the English. Some months later the French, who were by then at war with England, took those three river colonies with a force under the command of the Marquis de Lusignon. The French, whose two-year rule was a disagreeable one, built Fort Dauphin at the mouth of the Demerara and nearby began to build the new town of Longchamps. When the colony was restored to Holland in 1783 the Dutch chose Longchamps as the site of a new colonial capital to be called Stabroek, later to be renamed Georgetown by the British. Control of Guiana passed from nation to nation with the varying fortunes of the European Powers during the French Revolutionary and Napoleonic Wars. Guiana finally became British in 1815 by terms of the Treaty of Vienna.

In 1831 the colony of British Guiana was created by the union of Demerara, Essequibo and Berbice, with Georgetown as its administrative center. In 1833 an act of the British Parliament directed that slavery by abolished within five years' time. In 1837 John Gladstone suggested that in view of the departure of the Africans from the plantations, indentured laborers should be imported. Indentured servants came from Germany and England, Portuguese arrived from the island of Madeira, and still others came from Ireland, Malta and China. The largest number (238,960), however, came from India. Between 1838 and 1917 a total of 340,962 immigrants arrived in British Guiana.

The old plantocracy of Guiana received a crippling blow in 1846 with the passage of the Sugar Act which brought about a new levelling of the price of sugar so that the planters were in competition with other sugar producing countries, such as Cuba, that still used slave labor. The immigrant laborers, however, had brought with them an alternative crop to sugar—rice. It was their staple food and was grown on land not used by sugar plantations.

In 1917, as a result of the pressure of public opinion in India, the Government of India abolished the indenture system and no more Indian labor was allowed to enter the colony. The Indian population of British Guiana at that time was 126, 517; by 1938 it was 142, 736. In 1950 it had risen to 192,500 and by 1970 the total population of Indians was approximately 352,000. The number of Africans has also increased, but not at such a rapid rate. In 1921 there were 117,000 Africans; in 1952 there were 162,700; and by 1970 that number had risen to 212,300. In other words, while in 1917 there were only 9,000 more Indians than Africans in Guiana in 1970 the difference was 139,700.

In 1927 a commission reported on the British Guiana Constitution. The existing Constitution had provided for a bicameral division of legislative power between, on the one hand, the governor, seven appointed officials and eight elected unofficial members and, on the other hand, six elected members known as financial representatives. The purpose of the two chamber system was to divide legislation into a financial division controlled by the financial representatives and a non-financial division, dominated by the Governor and his "court of policy." In addition, there was an Executive Council headed by the Colonial Secretary and the Attorney-General. In executing his powers the Governor was bound to consult the Executive Council and if he acted against their advice on any matter he was compelled to give his reasons fully to the Secretary of State.

A new Constitution was adopted in 1928 which provided for a Legislative Council consisting of fifteen members appointed by the governor and fourteen members elected by the people. Nominated members were Europeans while elected members were of African and Asian descent. The electoral list of 1928 showed 11,000 voters in a population of 300,000. A constitutional change empowered the Governor to select two members from the elected group to serve in the executive branch.

Between 1928 and 1936 a series of strikes and riots occured in British Guiana. In 1938 a Royal Commission for the West Indies, known as the Moyne Commission, investigated social and economic conditions in the British territories of the Caribbean. Its full report was not published until 1945, and as a result of its findings, the British Government created a Colonial Development Fund for the West Indies.

A new Constitution came into effect in 1945, which established a Legislative Council comprised of the Governor, a Colonial Secretary, a Financial Secretary, the Attorney General, and five elected members. A change in the franchise gave all literate persons over 21 the right to vote, provided they were tenants of three acres of land, or owned land valued at $150.00, or had an annual income of $120.00.

As a result of an all-out war against malaria started after World War II, the population began to increase rapidly. The population was approximately 280,000 in 1945. Today it stands at more than 728,000. About 90% of the people live and work on the coastlands, a narrow belt including only 5% of the total area of the country.

In 1949, the People's Progressive Party (PPP) was formed. Its founders were Cheddi Jagan, a dentist; Forbes Burnham, a young London-educated lawyer; Mrs. Janet Jagan, an American; Ashton Chase, J. M. Hubbard, Sidney King, Rudy Luck and Martin Carter. The aims of the party were self-government, economic development, and social revolution.

In 1950, a three man Commission under the chairmanship of Sir E. J. Waddington, recommended the introduction of universal suffrage, thereby extending the vote to illiterate persons. The Commission also noted that candidates for election had often appealed to the electorate on racial grounds and added that it was imperative that racial preoccupations be banished if British Guiana were to progress. They suggested that it be made illegal for anyone to refer in an election speech to the racial origin of any candidate.

Early in 1953 a new Constitution, drawn up according to the recommendations of the Waddington Commission, was brought into being. Its salient features were:

(1) Universal suffrage;

(2) A bicameral legislature consisting of a House of Assembly, composed of twenty-four elected members and three ex-officio members (the Chief Secretary, the Attorney-General and the Financial Secretary) and a State Council composed of nine members appointed by the Governor;

(3) An Executive Council consisting of the Governor as President and three ex-officio members of the House of Assembly, six ministers chosen from among the elected members of the House of

Assembly and vested by the Governor with the charge of government departments;

(4) A Public Service Commission to advise the Governor on matters relating to the public services;

(5) The Governor to retain the usual powers.

On April 27, 1953, Guianese voters elected the PPP leaders Dr. Jagan and Mr. Burnham, and sixteen other members out of the twenty-four seats in the House of Assembly. As a result of strikes and the leftist leanings of the party leaders, the Constitution was suspended in September 1953. British troops were flown in from Jamaica and the Governor took over the government himself. An interim government was appointed by the Governor and the Colonial Office. It ruled from December 12, 1953 to August 21, 1957.

In 1955 the PPP split. There was a struggle for control of the Party between Dr. Jagan and Mr. Burnham. The members of the Party tended to identify with specific geographic areas and ethnic groups.

In 1957, the Constitution was restored and in the following elections both factions of the PPP ran candidates. Dr. Jagan's faction won nine seats, Mr. Burham's three seats, the National Labor Front led by Samuel Luckoo won one seat, and the United Democratic Party one seat.

A Constitutional conference on British Guiana was held in March, 1960 in London. Attending were representatives of all of the British Guianese political parties. Another constitution was adopted which accorded a large measure of responsibility to the majority in the Legislative Assembly, but the control of police, defense and external affairs remained with the Governor.

On August 21, 1961 elections were held for thirty-five seats. Dr. Jagan's PPP won twenty seats; the People's National Congress, led by Forbes Burnham, won eleven seats. Mr. Peter D'aquiar's United Force won four seats. Dr. Jagan then pressed the British to grant independence. The Colonial Office in London decided on a conference in May of 1962 to fix a date for independence.

On January 31, 1962, Dr. Jagan announced the need for $43,000,000 in additional revenue. Several new taxes were recommended, including a compulsory five percent per month saving scheme on personal income and ten percent per month on business income. On February 13, 1962, Guianese workers went on strike protesting the new legislation. On February 16, 1962, rioting and looting followed upon the outbreak of fire in Georgetown. Four city blocks were burned, damage was estimated at $28,000,000. Dr. Jagan was forced to withdraw his tax scheme.

On October 22, 1962, there was a constitutional conference on British Guiana in London. After a recess the meeting was resumed in 1963. At this conference, the three leaders, Dr. Jagan, Mr. Burnham and Mr. D'aquiar agreed to abide by the decisions of the Colonial Secretary, Mr. Duncan Sandys, who decided on porportional representation with the voting age to remain at twenty-one, and decided to defer fixing the date of independence.

On March 25, 1963, the official Gazette carried the draft of a Labor Relations Bill which gave the Minister of Labor the authority to issue certificates to recognize unions after supervised worker elections. Trade leaders asked that the bill be deferred. On April 18, 1963 the Trades Union Council decided on a strike which began on April 19th and lasted until July 6, 1963. The estimated cost was $4,500,000 in budget revenues and $2 million in wages lost. In April, 1963 the East Indians and Africans renewed race riots destroying many lives and property estimated at thousands of dollars. A strike called by a Jagan-backed union in February, 1964 caused further trouble.

The death toll approached 300 as the country prepared for elections on December 7, 1964, when 247,000 voters would decide which party would be in power under proportional representation. In the December election the PPP won 24 seats, the PNC won 22 seats and the United Force seven seats.

A PNC—UF coalition was formed with Forbes Burnham as Prime Minister. Another constitutional conference was held in London in November of 1965. Representatives of the three major parties were invited to attend but Dr. Jagan declined. The new constitution went into effect on May 26, 1966, the date of independence for the new state of Guyana.

Under the leadership of Burnham, and with British and American economic support, Guyana achieved modest progress. Based on this progress and the optimistic spirit engendered by independence, Burnham hoped for strong support in the next election of December, 1968. Forbes Burnham and the PNC did win an election victory and picked up six additional seats, but the election results were challenged on the grounds of fraud and corruption.

Since that date the country has ceased to make economic progress, primarily because what gains are made are more than offset by the rapid population growth. In order to try to solve his problems Burnham moved to remove the last vestiges of colonialism and on February 27, 1970, Guyana became the Cooperative Republic of Guyana. It remains to be seen how effective the new tenure will be.

GUYANA

A REVIEW OF RECENT POLITICAL DEVELOPMENTS

Harold A. Lutchman

Introduction

Few developing countries have embarked on the experience of independence under more difficult circumstances than Guyana. This former British colony, unlike her independent counterparts of the Commonwealth Caribbean, had to pass through a painful and drawn-out process before independence was finally achieved in May, 1966. After the breakup of the West Indian Federation, in 1962, independence for Jamaica was easily achieved, and once that precedent had been set, there was no difficulty in Trinidad and Tobago following suit. Though there was some doubt whether, because of her size, Barbados would have been allowed to attain independence, that doubt was soon dispelled when the British Government responded positively to that country's desire for independence.

In all three cases both the ruling parties and the opposition were in agreement on the form of the independence constitution, and, in some instances, both groups had also participated actively in bringing it into being. Although there was something of a crisis between the Government and Opposition in connection with the Trinidad and Tobago independence conference, this was resolved after what is sometimes regarded as an outstanding show of statesmanship on the part of the Leader of the Opposition, Dr. Capildeo. This development not only saved the conference but ensured that Government and Opposition in Trinidad and Tobago were in fundamental accord on the independence issue in August, 1962.

In Jamaica, which was the first to reach the goal of independence,

13

once the choice of the electorate between Federation and "going it alone" was made, Manley and Bustamante had no difficulty in proceeding to London to settle the final details of their independence constitution. There was no fundamental point of difference between the two parties. Very similar conclusions apply to Barbados.

On the other hand, Guyana achieved its independence in an atmosphere of crisis. The opposing People's Progressive Party (PPP) did not participate in the drafting of the country's independence Constitution, nor did it attend the independence conference. In fact, the PPP was bitterly opposed to the granting of independence to Guyana while the current Government was in power. The PPP contented that the Government was not legitimate because, among other things, it was brought to power by unfair means, and was in consequence not qualified to speak for the majority of Guyanese. In such circumstances the PPP felt that it alone should have been allowed to lead the country into independence. The PPP therefore adopted a posture of non-cooperation with the People's National Congress—United Force (PNC—UF) Coalition Government. Consequently, many observers arrived at the conclusion that Guyana was likely to witness a repetition of some of the unfortunate incidents of its recent past.

Elements In The Crisis

Ever since 1953, when Guyana received a relatively advanced Constitution including the grant of universal adult suffrage,[1] the country's political development had, with marked frequency, assumed crisis proportions. In that year the PPP, representing a coalition of the more progressive elements in the society, emerged as the dominant political force, and forged a sharp break in the pattern of the past. Unlike the leaders of the neighboring British West Indies, Guyana's leaders were not prepared to accept the slow evolutionary pattern of constititional development stipulated by the British as the path through which colonies had to pass in their march to

1. For the details of the Constitution, see *British Guiana: Report of the Constitutional Commission, 1950-51*, Colonial No. 280 (London: H.M.S.O., 1951).

independence. Rather, the approach of the leaders of the PPP was, from the very outset, revolutionary. They utilized the rhetoric of Marxism, communism and socialism, and adopted an anti-colonial and anti-imperialist attitude in their approach to, and examination of, the state of the society and its problems.[2] As was to be expected, that proved unacceptable to the British authorities who, within a period of six months of the PPP being in office, suspended the Constitution.[3] That act, in the view of scholars of Guyana's political development, was directly responsible for the succession of crises which ultimately became a feature of Guyanese life.

In 1955 the PPP separated into two hostile factions: one led by Forbes Burnham, and the other by Cheddi Jagan. Although this division was not originally along racial lines, the fact that these two persons were identified as the leaders of their respective racial groups, which constituted the major groups in Guyana, made it easy for such a development to occur.[4] Historical developments in Guyana had resulted in a situation capable of generating conflict between the two major groups. In the view of some observers, the PPP merely represented an uneasy alliance between East Indians and Negroes forged by their respective leaders as a means of presenting a common front to the colonial power.[5] The first serious crisis was therefore likely to disrupt this arrangement.

When a form of representative government was restored in 1957, the elections held in that year revealed a marked polarization of the electorate along racial lines, a pattern that continued until independence in May 1966. That, however, was only one manifestation of increasing racism in Guyana. A related development was the reluctance of the People's National Congress (the new name given to the Burnhamite faction of the PPP after its defeat at the 1957 general elections) to accept the new system of election. Its main objection was that the system was weighted permanently in favour of the PPP. The PNC therefore argued for a change to proportional representation, which it regarded as a far more equitable system.

2. *Report of the British Guiana Constitutional Commission, 1954*, Cmd. 9274 (London: H.M.S.O., 1954).

3. *Ibid.*

4. Raymond T. Smith, *British Guiana* (London: Oxford University Press, 1962), pp. 179, ff.

5. *Ibid.*, pp. 178, ff.

PNC demands for such a change were brought into sharper focus after the August 1961 elections.[6]

Those elections were held under a constitution intended to usher in self-government in Guyana[7] and were bitterly contested. As on the occasion of the 1957 general elections, the PPP alleged that the constituencies had been drawn with a view to ensuring PPP defeat.[8] Both parties also accused each other of using appeals to their respective racial groups as a means of achieving victory. There was the additional fact that the achievement of independence was a distinct possibility after the elections. All that remained for independence to become a reality was for the British Government to set a date for the transfer of control of external affairs to the local Government.

Of the 35 seats at stake in the 1961 elections, the PPP won 20, the PNC 11, and the newly-formed United Force four seats. The PNC was dissatisfied because, although it received approximately one per cent less votes than the PPP, there was a difference of nine in the seats won by the two parties. The contention was that with approximately 43% of the votes, the PPP constituted a minority party against the combined 41% (approximately) and 16% (approximately) won by the PNC and the UF, respectively. In summary, the general attitude of the other parties was one of challenge to the legitimacy of the PPP Government of Dr. Cheddi Jagan.[9]

Subsequent developments in Guyana by no means improved the relationship between the Government and its opposition. Within six months the Government was confronted with a serious crisis. The occasion was the presentation of the new Government's budget in February, 1962 which resulted in strikes, rioting, arson and loss of life.[10] Although it may be contended that the opposition parties, trade unions and other groups that reacted unfavorably to the budget were motivated by the feeling that its proposals were oppressive and anti-working class, there is also evidence to suggest that some of those groups were motivated by a desire to bring about

6. Forbes Burnham, *A Destiny To Mould,* comps. C.A. Nascimento and R. A. Burrowes (Longman Caribbean, 1970), pp. 14, ff.

7. For the details of the Constitution see, *Constitutional Instruments, 1961* (Government of British Guiana).

8. Cheddi Jagan, *The West on Trial* (London: Michael Joseph, 1966), pp. 14, ff.

9. Burnham, pp. 14, ff.

10. Jagan, chap. 12.

the defeat of the Government[11]. That result, however, was not achieved, partly because of the intervention of British troops.

At the constitutional conference held in October 1962, the Government and opposition parties failed to reach agreement on reform of the electoral system. Both the UF and the PNC argued in favour of a change to proportional representation, while the PPP supported the existing system. Further, the UF and PNC argued in favor of new elections before independence. The resulting deadlock precipitated the failure of the conference.[12]

The year 1963 witnessed the longest general strike in the history of Guyana. Its occasion was the attempt by the Government to enact a Labor Relations Bill designed to decide the recognition of trade unions in case of jurisdictional disputes.
According to Dr. Jagan's account, the bill was

opposed by the Trades Unions Council in alliance with: the two oppostion parties, the U.S. Central Intelligence Agency (C.I.A.), British Intelligence, big business, and the press. These various elements felt, soon after the publication of the bill that the time had come to bring down my Government.

The strike, which lasted 80 days, resulted in racial clashes between East Indians and Negroes, loss of life and destruction of property.[13]

The next year witnessed the most serious in the series of crises: a strike by Guyana Agricultural Workers Union, a PPP-backed union, in support of its demand for recognition as the bargaining agent for sugar workers. Opinions differ as to responsibility for that development. To some, it was sparked off by the PPP in an attempt to postpone the holding of elections under proportional representation in accordance with the decision of the British Government at the constitutional conference held in October 1963. There were to be new elections under proportional representation which would thereafter be the electoral system. This development spelled the defeat of the PPP, which therefore had to take steps to avert this

11. *Report of a Commission of Enquiry into Disturbances in British Guiana in February, 1962*, Col No. 354 (London: H.M.S.O., 1962), chap. 7; See also Jagan, chap. 12.
12. Jagan, pp. 267, ff.
13. *Ibid.*, pp. 272, ff.

eventuality. On the other hand, Dr. Jagan blamed his political opponents for the incidents. They, in his view, were bent on embarrassing his Government and bringing about its overthrow, with the collaboration of the British and American Governments.[14]

However, the results of the incidents were far more pertinent than the cause. Dr. Jagan summarizes the results of the strike as follows:

> The toll for the 1964 disturbances was heavy. About 2,668 families involving approximately 15,000 persons were forced to move their houses and settle in communities of their own ethnic group. The large majority were destroyed by fire. A total of 176 people were killed and 92 injured. Damage to property was estimated at about $4.3 million and the number of displaced persons we employed reached 1,342.[15]

The net effect of the events of 1964 was a worsening of race relations and a shift in those dissatisfied with the electoral system from the opposition to the governing party.

After the new elections, held in December 1964, although the PPP lost its previous majority, it refused to concede defeat and had to be removed from office by an amendment to the Constitution by the British Government. Even after this was effected, the PPP persisted for a long time in a policy of boycott of the Legislature and the activities of the PNC–UF Coalition Government.

Significant Developments Since Independence

Quite apart from the heritage of racial bitterness, political conflict, and the posture of the PPP, the Government, upon the achievement of independence, was confronted with other serious problems which largely prescribed the course it pursued. The fact that it was a coalition of two parties that differed on many fundamental issues weighed heavily against its chances of success. There was no secret that the coalition was the result of an "unholy alliance" created mainly to defeat the PPP, rather than a coalition founded on a

14. *Ibid.*, chap. 17.
15. *Ibid.*, p. 361

common policy or conviction, capable of pursuing a common line. In terms of ideology, the PPP and the PNC had more in common with each other than either had with the UF. While both of the former professed a form of socialism, the UF from its formation espoused a capitalist ideology. A coalition between the PPP and the PNC was therefore more likely to succeed than one between the UF and the PNC. Yet, contrary to expectations in some quarters, the coalition not only survived until independence and for some time thereafter, but its regime was accompanied by a period of peace in marked contrast to the previous years of PPP rule. The Government quite naturally claimed credit for those developments, in addition to asserting that it was responsible for a period of relative prosperity and improvement in race relations.[16]

In spite of the apparent improvements, there remained a keen awareness that on the achievement of independence there had been much uneasiness on the part of the East Indian section of the population, a group that tended to regard the Government as one dominated by the Negro-led PNC. Although in theory there was a coalition in power, there is little doubt that the Government was in fact dominated, both in terms of membership and influence, by the PNC. After a time, the operative expression, in so far as PNC ministers were concerned, became not "the PNC–UF Government", but the "PNC-led Government."

While in power the policy of the PNC was quite simple. It took credit for everything praiseworthy while blaming its failures on the fact that it was hamstrung by being in coalition with the UF. There was therefore little surprise when, on the eve of the general elections held in December 1968, most of the UF ministers resigned from the Government. The PNC did not, however, lose office since it had successfully induced some members of the PPP and the UF to "cross the floor". The issue on which the Coalition broke up was that of the "Representation of the People's Bill" which was designed to provide legislation for the general elections. The split came in October 1968.

The elections of December 1968 were, like so many held previously, conducted in the midst of controversy. On this occasion, the main points of dissatisfaction on the part of the opposition

16. Burnham, pp. 48, ff.

parties were the questions of overseas voting, the introduction of the alphabet systems, the system of proxy voting and the manner in which it was used. The first issue referred to the arrangement under which persons of Guyanese citizenship living overseas were eligible to vote, while the second matter concerned the choice of candidates under the list system of proportional representation. Under the old arrangement, when each party submitted its list, it was required to indicate its preference of candidates, but under the proposed new arrangement a party could submit the names of its candidates in any order. After the elections, it was then left to the party to choose its representatives from the list, in accordance with the number of seats to which it was entitled.

All these proposals were criticised by the opposition. They regarded the overseas voting proposal merely as a device on the part of the PNC to perpetuate itself in office by unfair means. The PPP in particular argued that there was no justification for persons who, in many instances, had no meaningful connection with Guyana to have the right to participate in the election of a Government in equal measure with those who lived in Guyana and paid their taxes in the country. The main retort of the PNC was that there were ample precedents for "overseas voting" and that in any case there was an adequate constitutional and legal basis for the arrangement.

The second proposal was criticised mainly on the grounds that it was undemocratic and robbed the electorate of the democratic right to elect candidates of their choice. Further, it was likely to lead to dictatorial tendencies since, in the final analysis, the choice of representatives would be made by one man—the leader of a party. The PNC contended, however, that it was merely giving expression to what was already a reality in Guyanese politics, the dominance of parties. It was useless to pretend that the electorate in Guyana voted for individuals and not party, which was, in the final analysis, responsible to the electorate. Consequently, regardless of the candidates finally chosen for membership of the legislature, the party's responsibility to the electorate was preserved.

The proxy system was particularly criticized after the election results revealed a clear victory for the PNC. The results revealed that the PNC had defeated the PPP in some areas traditionally regarded as the latter's strongholds. The opposition was especially perturbed by the fact that the number of votes cast by proxy were neither known nor published, and they alleged that the Government had used the system effectively to rig the elections. They were also critical of the contribution which the overseas votes made in returning the PNC to office.

The breakdown of the votes at the general elections was as follows:

PNC	174,339	(55.81%)
PPP	113,991	(36.48%)
UF	23,162	(7.42%)
GUMP	899	(.29%)
	312,391	

The allocation of seats was as follows:

PNC	30
PPP	19
UF	4
	53

The PNC argued that the swing in its favor merely represented a response to the period of peace and prosperity that followed its accession to office. The electorate was convinced by its argument that, if returned to office with a large majority, the PNC would do much more than as part of a coalition. The PNC further contended that it was only because the PPP was racial in outlook, and regarded East Indians as its exclusive preserve, that the PPP could not accept that even East Indians could have responded to the PNC's appeal. The proxy system, it submitted, was designed to ensure that persons who wanted to vote in favor of a particular party could do so without fear of intimidation.

Rather than entering into a discussion of the values of the conflicting claims and counterclaims of the Government and its opponents, it is of far more importance to identify some of the consequences that flowed from those criticisms and feelings. Particular regard should be paid to the attitude of the PPP in the matter. If nothing else, the PPP seemed confirmed in the view that it could not extend unqualified recognition to, and regard as legitimate, a Government formed by the PNC. This attitude was ambivalent, however, since the PPP seemed to be confronted with a dilemma which is still very much a feature of Guyanese politics. If it should, for example, pursue a consistent policy of obstruction and opposition to the Government, there is little doubt that such a policy would have any more than a marginal effect (if any) on the Government's position. Apart from the fact that the PNC has the necessary majority in Parliament to give effect to its policies, the PNC, unlike the PPP when in office, is not confronted with a hostile trade union movement and civil service.[17] Further, it is unlikely that supporters of the PPP would look favorably on a situation in which they are without representation in Parliament. There are probably some party members who would also think twice before they willingly agree to forego the prestige and income attached to the post of Member of Parliament. Then there is the recognition that Parliament, despite the limited purposes which some believe it serves, nevertheless provides a forum which could be used for criticizing and exposing the Government. For these and other reasons the PPP participates in government although it may still adopt a posture and use rhetoric designed to suggest its nonrecognition of the Government.

There are those who believe that the PPP now represents a spent force in Guyanese politics. Those who subscribe to this view generally base their evaluation in part on the belief that the PNC Government has succeeded in gaining support among those once regarded as favorably disposed to Dr. Jagan and the PPP. They further contend that as Prime Minister, Forbes Burnham has demonstrated outstanding qualities of leadership and has been fairly effective in winning, if not support, co-operation from a wide cross-section of the population. In particular, quite a few of his former opponents have rallied around him, and some serve in high positions with his Government. The PPP on the other hand, the theory goes, has been fairly ineffective and is in relative disarray.

In a sense, developments along those lines were to be expected. It often occurs that, on losing office, the leader of a party finds that there is an accompanying decline in his authority and influence, while the leader of the party winning office experiences an increase

17. For a useful account of the role of the Civil Service under the PPP Government see, Bertram Collins, "The Civil Service of British Guiana in the General-Strike of 1963," *Caribbean Quarterly* 10, no. 2 (July 1965).

in his authority and influence. The position of the former can be bolstered by a judicious use of the patronage which is then at the disposal of the Government party.

There are other elements in the Guyanese circumstances which are likely to influence these developments. One of the consequences of the alphabet system of proportional representation is its effect on the authority of the leaders of parties. That system, which bases the choice of legislators on party membership, enhances the position of the leaders, since they can exercise their choice so as to ensure that those selected are willing to follow the party line without question. It is difficult for individuals, save perhaps the leader of a party, to enjoy personal support from a particular constituency as was sometimes the case under the earlier electoral system.[18] These facts, in part, explain the tendency for "yes men" to be well represented among the legislators. There is no doubt that within recent times the caliber of those selected as Members of Parliament has undergone a significant change, and that candidates are being chosen from a wider range of persons and occupations than previously.[19]

A concommitant development is the infrequency with which Parliament meets, and very often, as the opposition alleges, it is only summoned when it suits the purposes of the Government. Further, there is a tendency to make and announce important decisions outside of Parliament in circumstances in which its approval is taken for granted. In short, there has been a relative decline in the importance and role of Parliament.

In accounting for these developments, some regard should be paid to the fact that there has recently been a serious questioning of the revelance of certain institutions in Guyanese society. One of these is the role of, and need for, a political opposition. Some persons contend that while this system works well in the United Kingdom where the opposition is required to, and does, play a constructive role in government, in a country like Guyana the opposition tends to oppose for the sake of opposing and is inclined to be destructive in its activities. In such circumstances, a great deal of time and

18. It was believed that W.O.R. Kendall was, under the first-past-the-post system, capable of winning in New Amsterdam in his own right and without regard to party connection.

19. One of the outstanding features is that few backbenchers now intervene in debates in the National Assembly.

valuable resources, which could otherwise be better utilized, are uselessly dissipated.

Beyond Independence

The Prime Minister, in a recent address to the nation, stated that on taking office in December 1965, he and his colleagues had promised to achieve three objectives:

(1) The establishment of peace and tranquillity after years of internecine strife;

(2) The achievement of political independence;

(3) The winning of economic independence and bringing of social justice to the masses.

He submitted that the first two objectives have already been achieved but the third remains outstanding.[20]

The PNC contends that from the outset it had been anti-colonial and stood for the removal of all the vestiges of colonialism from Guyanese society. While it was part of the Coalition Government, it was prevented from taking effective action to complete the process of decolonization, even after the achievement of independence in May 1966. At the Independence Conference of November 1965, the PNC declared in favor of a republic as part of the process of decolonization, but was thwarted by the UF which favored a monarchic system. Provision was, however, made in the Constitution for the possibility of change after January 1, 1969.[21]

During the 1968 election campaign, the PNC stated that if returned to power, it would take measures to effect the constitutional changes necessary to make Guyana a republic. As a result, in August 1969, the Government gave notice of its intention to establish what it described as the first "Co-operative Republic" in the world on February 23, 1970.[22] In sum, the PNC represents an

20. Burnham, "Guyana's Bauxite" (Broadcast address to the Nation by the Prime Minister, November 28, 1970).

21. Burnham, "Towards A Co-operative Republic" (Address to the 12th Congress of the People's National Congress, *Daily Chronicle, Ltd.*, 1969).

22. Harold A. Lutchman, "The Co-operative Republic of Guyana" *Caribbean Studies* 10 no. 3 (October 1970). For a more detailed account of the objectives of the Co-operative Republic see, *Co-operative Republic of Guyana, 1970* (Ministry of Information, Georgetown, 1970).

attempt to end the colonial relationships and values which still persist and affect Guyana, in addition to achieving rapid economic development through self-reliance. Particular emphasis is to be placed on the ideal of "making the small man a real man."[23] According to the Government, there is an interconnection between political independence and economic independence because without economic independence "political independence is in jeopardy, if not meaningless, since our economy will continue to be subject to the interests and manipulations of outsiders."[24]

Consequently, Guyana has lately assumed a position of prominence in the movement for Caribbean integration. As a publication of the Government states:

> A commitment to Caribbean unity is one of the main features of Guyana's foreign policy. Thus, the Prime Minister. . . . .within a few weeks of his assumption of office, in December, 1964, took the initiative in establishing closer links with the other Caribbean territories. Such action led directly to the signing in December, 1965, of an Agreement with Barbados and Antigua to establish CARIFTA—the Caribbean Free Trade Area. This Agreement marked the important beginning of a new movement towards economic integration.[25]

From this very modest beginning, CARIFTA has expanded to include all the independent and Associated States in the Commonwealth Caribbean. In addition, other agencies such as the Regional Secretariat and the Caribbean Development Bank, have materialized as important elements in the movement towards greater Caribbean integration. Further, a number of conferences have been convened from time to time with a view to achieving co-operation between the states of the Commonwealth Caribbean on a wide range .of subjects.[26]

The question of Caribbean integration is regarded as crucial to the process of decolonization in Guayana and in making its indepen-

23. *Co-operative Republic of Guyana, 1970.*
24. Burnham, "Guyana's Bauxite."
25. *Guyana Journal* 1, no. 1 (April 1968): 5.
26. *Guyana Journal* 1, no. 2 (December 1968); 1, no. 3 (December 1969); 1, no. 4 (September 1970).

dence meaningful, because of the recognition that individual states cannot achieve improvement in their circumstances unless they pool the resources of their small economies. The alternative, it is argued, is a perpetuation of dependence on either those who once served or who still serve the former "Mother Country". There is also the very important problem of multi-national corporations whose activities cut across national boundaries and therefore require a measure of co-operation among the states of the region. In the absence of such co-operation, the corporations can successfully manipulate the states in the direction they choose.

Guyana not only favors integration on the economic plane, but would also like to see progress achieved in the political sphere. Although the achievements so far are noteworthy, there are serious difficulties in the way of moving toward political integration, because failure of the last Federation has left West Indian leaders particularly wary of any development in that direction.[27]

Guyana also favors throwing open its doors to West Indians.[28] This policy is justified on the grounds that the country possesses large expanses of unoccupied land, while her sister nations in the region tend to be over-populated. There is a marked imbalance in the distribution of the population even within the borders of Guyana, since the great masses of the people are located on the coastlands while the interior is relatively underpopulated. This occurred because of the deliberate policy of those who controlled the country's affairs during the colonial era. In an attempt to off-set this imbalance, the Government has recently initiated a policy of encouraging Guyanese to settle in the interior.[29] The success of this "thrust into the interior" is impressive, and it has been stimulated by construction of a road designed to link Guyana with Brazil. These developments are viewed with suspicion by certain sections of the East Indian population which see, behind the policy of encouraging West Indians to settle in Guyana, a design to upset the majority which they now possess in population.

27. Michael Manley, "Overcoming Insularity in Jamaica," *Foreign Affairs* 49, no. 1 (October 1970).

28. *Guyana Journal* 1, no. 1 (April 1968): 62, ff.

29. The policy of "interior development" or settlement was in large measure influenced by the border problems with which the country was confronted. See Burnham, *"Towards A Co-operative Republic,"* in which the Prime Minister emphasized that "defence and security can be combined with development."

Some of the most significant political developments in Guyana since independence have occurred in the field of the country's international relations. The challenges which the country has had to face in this sphere dramatize the difficult circumstances under which it became independent. Those challenges also in large measure determined the course of developments in Guyana. It is perhaps unlikely that the country would have been so active in international forums had it not been confronted with serious border problems with its neighbours. The extent of the problems facing the newly independent state may be seen from the fact that the Venezuelan claim alone amounted to an area of approximately 53,000 square miles, or more than half the total area of Guyana. In such circumstances, Guyana's foreign policy, unlike that of her neighbors of the Commonwealth Caribbean, had of necessity to be conditioned primarily by the objective of survival as a nation. The country's plight was compounded by the fact that the British had left no heritage of meaningful relations between Guyana and her neighbors.

Although there has as yet been no systematic study of Guyana's foreign policy, there is little doubt that Guyana has been successful in this field. The country has achieved a measure of accord with both Venezuela and Surinam, in addition to establishing friendly relations with Brazil, her neighbor to the South. The most significant recent development in this field has been the Protocol of Port of Spain concluded between Guyana and Venezuela on June 18th, 1970.[30] The Minister of State for Foreign Affairs recently informed the United Nations that "If the opportunities it provides are grasped, if the possibilities it offers are pursued, this Protocol will represent an achievement for the methods of the conference table in an anniversary year that. . . .has recorded all too few successes of this kind."[31] The Protocol provides for a minimum period of 12 years during which Venezuela undertakes not to assert any claim to sovereignty over the Essequibo Region of Guyana, while Guyana will assert no claim to Venezuelan territory. Both governments also agree to promote a closer understanding between their peoples.[32]

30. *Guyana Journal* 1, no. 4, pp. 87, ff.

31. S. S. Ramphal, "Peace—Justice—Progress: The International Imperatives" (Address delivered in the General Assembly at the Special Commemorative Session marking the 25th Anniversary of the United Nations, Ministry of External Affairs, Georgetown, October 21, 1970), p. 14.

32. *Guyana Journal* 1, no. 4.

Although the opposition has been critical of the Protocol, there is a wide feeling in Guyana that it represents a triumph for the Government and the people of Guyana.

Conclusion

In the view of some observers, despite many encouraging developments, there is still a great deal of discontent and dissatisfaction below the surface of Guyanese society. Although there is little doubt that Forbes Burnham and his PNC Government feel themselves the masters of the situation, in Guyana there remains the view that they recognize that there is no room for complacency, and that national unity is still an objective to be achieved. Evidence of the confidence of the Government may be seen from the fact that there was no hesitation on their part in permitting the Black Power leader, Stokely Carmichael, to visit Guyana early in 1970, at a time when other Commonwealth Caribbean states were refusing him entry to their territories. Further, the Government has initiated action on such "radical" proposals as diplomatic relations with the U.S.S.R. and the acquisition of majority shares in the bauxite industry. In fact, the Government has announced its intention of acquiring 51% ownership in all the major industries in the country. Both of these measures are likely to be unpalatable to some interests, both inside and outside of Guyana, and have an adverse effect on the flow of investment funds and assistance to Guyana. The Burnham Government does not, however, seem unduly perturbed by the latter possibility, since it emphasizes that the main plank of its policy is self-help, i.e. to develop Guyana by mobilizing its own resources.

The Prime Minister recently made the following significant statement:

We look back with pride at the change that had come about since the communal violence and animosities of the early sixties. But is that enough? Are there not still too many suspicious and smouldering antipathies, whose very existence point to potential weakness in the national fabric and give hope to unscrupulous and frustrated political helots?[33]

33. *Guyana Graphic*, January 1, 1970.

In the same context, the Prime Minister declared 1971 to be "Consolidation Year and the Year of National Unity." One of Guyana's newspapers, commenting on the significance of that declaration, pointed out that it would be hopeless to sow the grains of racism and discrimination and to expect to reap national harmony and cooperation. It would "be self-destructive to harbour the weeds of corruption." The newspaper also pointed to the unfortunate fact of there still being "a sizeable section of the community which carries politics into every field of endeavour in the country. . . ."[34]

These statements and others refer to what may be described as some unhealthy aspects of Guyanese politics. Chief among them are frequent and recurring allegations of malpractices at elections, and corruption in other aspects of Guyanese public life. Thus, the PPP has accused the Government of "destroying the democratic institutions of the country, posing a threat to parliamentary democracy by the continuous rigging of elections and political interference with the judiciary and armed forces."[35] In connection with the local government elections held in December 1970, the UF protested against what it described as "the latest example of electoral manipulation" which seemed "to be part of his [Burnham's] attempt to obtain absolute power while pretending to retain the principle of democracy."[36] In the view of certain sections of the population hostile to the Government, their fears were justified when, shortly after the return of the Prime Minister from his African tour late last year, there was displayed at a meeting of the Women's Auxiliary of his Party a banner calling for a One Party State. The Prime Minister, however, made a statement denying that there was any such intention on the part of his Government.

One of the first acts of the government in 1971 was to announce moves "to stamp out corruption and all malpractices in the public sector." The Prime Minister expressed concern against what he described as "the emergence of a threat to the development of our country and to the people of Guyana." In more specific terms, he referred to:

the efforts of some people actuated by ill will . . . and others spurred on by avarice and a selfish desire to use our newly-won

34. *Weekend Post and Sunday Argosy,* January 3, 1971.
35. *Sunday Graphic,* October 18, 1970.
36. *Sunday Graphic,* November 15, 1970.

independence to corrupt and so demoralize the nation and stultify its growth. With our determination to control our resources, there has been and will continue to be, attempts to deflect us from our purpose and to sabotage our efforts.[37]

Those attempts, according to the Prime Minister, took many forms including ". . . tempting holders of public office, political and civil service . . . to be involved in corrupt transactions or unethical practices."

The Prime Minister declared that his Government has set "its face firmly against all forms of corruption and all malpractices and will do everything to stamp them out. . . . Those whose privilege it is to serve in the public sector . . . must be free from venality of any kind. . . ." In consequence, he has consulted with the Ombudsman ("whose post is one under the Constitution and not subject to control by any other person or public office holder") with a view to his investigating complaints by any citizen of corruption, or attempts at corruption of, or by, officers who are paid from public funds. If the allegations are established, "they will be the basis of criminal proceedings and disciplinary and other action at the administrative level." Mr. Burnham also announced the intention of promulgating a "code of conduct and behaviour for Government Ministers and my Party Parliamentarians" for the information of the people.[37]

There is the belief in some quarters that the Prime Minister's statement would do a great deal to allay some of the fears, criticisms and rumors heard among certain sections of the Guyanese population that many persons, holding public office, were using their positions to enrich themselves. The opposition PPP, however, is not satisfied that the Government has gone far enough in its proposals. The PPP contends that the Government has done "too little too late . . . the procedures proposed to cope with the situation—the Ombudsman and the police—cannot and will not prove adequate." According to the PPP," if the P.[rime] M.[inister] is really serious about corruption, then the problem must be tackled not administratively but politically." It therefore calls for the appointment of a:

> top-level national Committee made up of Government and Opposition which will examine from top to bottom, from the

37. *Guyana Graphic,* January 5, 1971.

Prime Minister and Leader of the Opposition to the Village coun-
cillor and community organizer. Regional sub-committees—watch-
dog committees so called, should examine every nook and corner,
every public work, every public office and politician.

The PPP declared that it referred not only to corruption "in the sense
of stealing and accepting bribes. We also refer to political corruption. . . ."[38]

There is little doubt that given the will and sincerity to do so,
corruption and malpractices can be rooted out in any society,
including that of Guyana. However, the problem likely to be
perpetuated, and to remain a source of concern, if not conflict, in
Guyana is the electoral system. It is perhaps unnecessary to state that
there can never be a stable situation when groups competing for
power in a given polity are not in agreement on the rules by which
the game is to be played. In such circumstances, as may be seen from
events in Guyana's recent past, it invariably occurs that attempts are
made by those who consider that the system is weighted against
them to effect changes in the status quo. At the same time, those
who achieve success through the existing system always fight for its
preservation. One of the serious problems likely to pose a challenge
to Guyanese society in the future is that of averting a clash between
those two interest groups and of arriving at a situation in which all
parties agree on the rules. In the absence of a solution it may well be
that some of the events of the past might be repeated with very
serious consequences for the national interest. Guyana can by no
means achieve the rapid progress it seeks in the face of national
divisions and political disagreements of a fundamental nature.

38. *Evening Post,* January 5, 1971.

GUYANA

PRESENT POLITICAL SITUATION*

Brian Wearing

In the December 1964 elections the Peoples Progressive Party won 24 seats, the Peoples National Congress Party 22, and the United Force Party seven.[1] A PNC-UF coalition government was formed with Linden Forbes Sampson Burham, leader of the PNC, as Prime Minister. Thus, whilst it had been Dr. Cheddi Jagan who led the fight for independence, a fact acknowledged today in Guyana by supporters of both the PNC and UF, it was to be under Forbes Burnham's leadership that Guyana would be allowed its independence. The coalition was unlikely to last for long, combining as it did the left of centre PNC, and UF, backed by important sectors of the local business community and unashamedly capitalistic. Fear of Jagan was the only bond. However, despite a consciousness of the difficulties of its typical "colonial" economy, (sugar and bauxite exported and food and other necessities imported) the Guyanese demonstrated a great faith in their future. Everyone in Georgetown today still seems completely confident that there *must* be rich resources in the nation's vast hinterland, and they assume that it is

* This report is intended as a brief examination of the recent development of Guyana, and an assessment of the current situation, in an attempt to "up date" the study of the then British Guiana conducted by the Caribbean Institute and Study Center for Latin America (CISCLA) of the Inter American University of Puerto Rico in 1964.

Financial support by Inter American University allowed the writer to visit Guyana during August 1970: Whilst many interviews were initiated, especially valuable were those held with Her Excellency Mrs. Winifred Gaskin and Mr. Martin Carter, participants in the original institute held in October 1964. Mrs. Gaskin is now Guyana's High Commissioner for the Commonwealth Caribbean in Jamaica. Mr. Martin W. Carter is Minister of Information. Opinions were sought from senior members of the governing Peoples National Congress party, the Peoples Progressive party, and the United Force party. Discussions were held also with representatives from the fields of business and education.

1. One UF and three PPP members resigned from their respective parties but retained their seat in the House. Mr. d'Aguiar (UF) resigned from the cabinet in 1967.

simply a matter of time before those resources can be used to bring great prosperity to Guyana.

With British and American support Burnham achieved modest gains, and London became the site of a constitutional conference called in November 1965. Although the three parties represented in the Assembly were all invited to attend, Jagan and his PPP declined to do so. The resultant constitution came into effect on Independence Day, May 26th 1966. Burnham was now free to guide the destiny of the new nation, and perhaps to shed some light on his enigmatic personality. Would he prove, as many of his supporters believed, that he was the only man in Guyanese politics with the ability to create a political and social consensus, or was his wonderful wit and casual humor a mask for a potential dictatorship?

During the campaign for the December 1968 elections, Burnham claimed that in four years the intercommunal violence of the previous era had almost disappeared. Per capita income had risen from G$407 to G$480, and the country stood ready to benefit from the recent birth of CARIFTA. With over US$43 million in aid funds he had been able to build 380 miles of highway (including the controversial 44 mile Mackenzie Road), a new airport terminal building, rural water systems, many new schools, and an educational extension programme. In addition, the PNC had made overtures to the Indian population: Guyana now had a branch of the Bank of Baroda, national holidays had been declared on Muslim and Hindu festivals, government research aid was directed towards improving rice growing, and some government positions were given, with much publicity, to Indians.

On the other hand, the PPP leadership was split ideologically, with Jagan leading the "pro-Moscow" faction. Strangely, there had been no great dissent when its congress declared for Marxism-Leninism in August of 1968. The UF had emerged from the coalition relationship with a sullied image, and was vulnerable to the opponents' gibes that it was a "spent force." Even d'Aguiar's traditional anti-communist attacks were muted by his new dislike of Burnham.

Yet, the outstanding characteristic of this election was to be the taint of fraud and corruption. Both the PPP and UF complained bitterly about the "padding" of the electoral role, and tried to have the election postponed. Equally contentious was the question of the overseas vote. Burnham's international reputation was badly tarnished by the exposed discrepancies in the list of Guyanese voters in Great Britain. Ninety-seven percent of the overseas vote went to the PNC, giving it six additional seats. True, in Guyana it already had a clear majority of one, but here too there was substantial evidence of fraud. Many PNC supporters still feel guilty about this episode, and uneasily confess the opinion that despite his obvious talent, the Prime Minister obtained his position through Duncan Sandy's expedient of changing the voting system, and maintained it by even more questionable devices.[2]

Now, the future of Guyana became very dependent upon the manner in which Forbes Burnham exercised his control under new one party phase. Having blamed his previous shortcomings on the handicap of an alliance with the conservative UF, he now gained the opportunity to fulfill his promise of a truly national government.

It was toward this end that on February 27, 1970, Guyana became the Cooperative Republic of Guyana. There were two basic results from this action. First, the eradication of the "colonial mentality" which Burnham claims has dogged the area since British Guiana was made a crown colony in 1814. Second, it was to weld the people into a "self-help development programme based on a national system of cooperative ventures." This represents the Guyanese attempt to add a cooperative sector to the private and public sectors.

In Guyana itself, in mid 1970, there appeared to be not only a quiet confidence that the nation "was on the move," but a fair consensus as to what the direction should be. Here again, Guyana probably owes a debt to Cheddi Jagan, since even if his extremism is not acceptable to the majority of the people, all have heard him preach for so long that he has conditioned them to accept a high degree of socialism, and he has ironically made Burnham's task that much easier. However, the difficulty still seems to be the question of

2.

| | 1968 | | 1964 | |
	votes	seats	votes	seats
PNC:	174,214	30	96,651	22
PPP:	113,861	19	109,332	24
UF:	23,161	4	29,617	7

Of 36,745 votes cast overseas in 1968, PNC received 34,429; UF 1,053; PPP 1,003. The PNC percentage poll rose from 40.5% in 1964 to 56%. The PPP's percentage fell from 45.9% to 36.8%.

which group is going to guide the course of the future—Guyanese of African or Indian descent.

No matter what subjects were raised in the interviews, they always seemed to return to the question of the racial division of Guyana.[3] Mr. Carter stated bluntly that "the basis and crux of politics in Guyana is race." He did go on to emphasize the need to solve the unemployment problem, and this issue was stressed by several civil servants who placed economic factors at the head of their priority list. These men also stressed the PNC idea of "economic indepen-dence," and usually quoted the Prime Minister's parliamentary speech where he insisted that:

> Serious and earnest effort should be made to establish firmly and irrevocably the cooperative as a means of MAKING THE SMALL MAN A REAL MAN and changing, in a revolutionary fashion, the social and economic relationships to which we have been heir as part of our monarchical legacy.

Some government officials did, however, hint that the normally PNC supporting trade unions were becoming somewhat wary of the trend, and were disturbed by the potential growth in executive power.

PNC supporters are quick to take credit for the obvious decrease in violence under Forbes Burnham, and Guyanese of all races and political allegiance say that the pre-independence riots were a chastening experience which they do not wish to repeat. Yet an interesting feature of interviews with government officials of African descent was that whilst they stressed that there was a growing racial cooperation in politics, they did not notice a complementary cultural integration. Indeed, they did not welcome such a move and their

---

3. Population of Guyana: December 1967, the last year for which detailed estimated figures are available (Guyana Handbook 1970-71):

East Indians	352,000
Africans	212,300
Mixed	84,500
Chinese	44,400
Portuguese	6,200
Other European	1,200
Amerindian	32,180
TOTAL	692,780

The population was increasing at an annual rate of 3% at this time.

arguments against racial integration betrayed an appalling ignorance of the customs and attitudes of fellow Guyanese. PNC officials may believe that they will gain a multi-racial support for their political program without an integrated Guyanese society. The situation in Guyana today would seem to make that a debatable issue. Certainly, the oft-repeated assertion by Black government officials that they were western in outlook compared to the Indian Guyanese who are oriental and "less progressive" in their thinking, was not supported by the observations of the writer, who detected many signs that the young Guyanese of Indian descent are decidedly western in custom and thought.

Although there is almost unanimous Indian admiration for his past achievements, a few Indians suggested that Jagan had outlived his usefulness, and that the PPP's only chance for success would be to admit a Black Guyanese element into its leadership. By the far the most common reaction of well-educated Indians, however, was that they were willing and often enthusiastic about supporting the PNC, if only it would abandon its discriminatory appointment policy. PNC officials admitted that there was discrimination and extensive use of patronage. Sometimes they qualified their admission with the excuse "Well, Jagan started it." Many Guyanese, of all parties, feel that the PNC buys off political opponents, and were keen to quote the example of the recent municipal elections. There, Indian candidates swung their allegiance from the PPP to the PNC, along with charges of foul play over the question of proxy voting. One senior government official was quite cynical and contemptuous of PPP men who transferred their allegiance, because, "that is where the gravy is."

Dr. Jagan, as might be expected, emphasised that the PPP was appealing to, and educating, the black worker in an effort to convince him that the issue was one of class and not race. He admitted that the change might come through peaceable free elections. It was strange to hear Jagan extolling the virtues of the British system of electoral control and pleading for the retention of the right to appeal to a high court in Great Britain. Should violence erupt again, he stands ready to blame the increasingly restrictive policy and denial of honest elections by Forbes Burnham and the imperialist powers who support him. Typically, he regards the recent revival and temporary settlement of the boundary dispute with

Venezuela as demonstrating the United States hold over Guyana. He argues that Burnham knows that should he do anything to offend Washington, then the United States will threaten to unleash Venezuela upon him. This would make for an interesting situation for Burnham, should it occur, since he seems determined to acquire a controlling interest in the bauxite industry, owned by U.S. and Canadian interests.[4]

The UF sees its role as a "continuing presence," that the Guyanese people can turn to should they become disillusioned with the present Government, and want an alternative to the revolutionary change and violence that they expect should the PPP regain power. UF officials take great pains to point out that theirs is a multi-racial executive, and deny that it is a Portuguese dominated, middle class business party. It believes itself to be the champion of the Amerindian, no doubt prompted by the interests of the party's ex-leader Peter d'Aguiar. In line with PPP protests, UF also thinks that the much-publicized "New Era" proposed for the Amerindians by the PNC government is simply a means to gain political control over the indigenous population.

It seems that with the position gained in the 1968 elections, Forbes Burnham has been able to develop a strong controlling hand in Guyana. A steady move towards a one-party system is beginning, and the demoralization of the opposition that such a policy implies is noticeable. Restrictions on travel, both within Guyana and to overseas destinations, have had a strong psychological impact. Doubtless UF can argue that it has little chance under the present electoral system, but nevertheless it is in no position to offer effective opposition. With the majority of the nation's population of Indian descent, the PPP still has the potential for gaining the mass vote. But divided ideology, desertions, and the seeming hopelessness

4. In a broadcast to the nation on November 28th, 1970 the Prime Minister, Mr. Forbes Burnham, referred to three principal objectives which he had set on December 14, 1964, on assuming office as head of the Government of Guyana, then British Guiana; the establishing of peace and tranquillity, the achievement of political independence, and the winning of economic independence as a means of consolidating political independence and bringing social justice to the masses. Mr. Burnham stated, "The first and second objectives are now matters of fact, but the third is yet to be gained. Without it, political independence is in jeopardy if not meaningless. But a nation cannot achieve economic independence unless it owns and controls its resources, unless the decisions with respect to these resources are taken within its own borders."

of ever beating the Government at the ballot box, lessens its effectiveness.

If this assessment of the opposition is correct, Burnham stands a good chance of making good his intent to be Prime Minister for twenty years. He has controlled violence, because he exercises close control over the police and the army. The Guyanese army is too young to have developed a role as a politically conscious elite. It still has an obvious professional legacy from Great Britain, but the Prime Minister keeps a careful eye on officer selection, and consequently many dismiss as ridiculous the idea of a military coup. Nevertheless recent events in Trinidad came as a shock, and there are some who feel that the army is not entirely happy with the trend, and may yet take part in the political field.

At present, however, the Prime Minister will lose power only through major defections within the PNC. Patronage is used to surround him with sympathetic lieutenants. Possible challengers within the Party may find themselves switched to appointments that keep them out of the limelight. Without doubt, Forbes Burnham is a talented man with vision and ambition. Thus, as he gains strength within his own country he sees himself painting on a wider canvas than Guyana alone. His moral exhortation, strangely reminiscent of Cuba, was symbolized by his recent tree cutting adventures. The presence of students from other parts of the West Indies, "the leaders of tomorrow," on this project to build a road link between Guyana and Brazil, was an invaluable stimulus to his build-up as a Caribbean leader. His handling of Stokely Carmichael's visit also tended to show him as a man confident in his position, as opposed to some other Caribbean national leaders.

Burnham seems to consider himself a philosopher-economist who believes that it is the small man who controls political power, but that economic power is in the hands of foreign corporations. Thus his aim is to transfer economic power to those who now have political power. The people will have control over the ownership of the large corporations, and, second, by creating cooperatives, the small man will be able to participate in large scale enterprises. Since economic independence can only be achieved through international enterprise, Guyana will need to cooperate with similarly placed countries against the multi national corporations. This explains much of Burnham's regional approach, and his recent extensive tour of

African nations. Indeed, for a small nation of limited resources, Guyana envisages and is undertaking a heavy diplomatic commitment.

In Guyana, the suggestion that the Guyanese had any similarity with Latin Americans always brought a quick denial, though officials at the New Amsterdam Conference on Foreign Policy acknowledged that there are shared problems with Brazil that they hope can be solved in the light of mutual experience in a mood of cooperation. The difference in racial background, the British as opposed to Iberian colonial legacy, historical experience, and other points are noted and accepted. But the problems of social division, communications, exploitation of natural resources, tendency to have political elites based on racial and cultural factors are some examples that suggest that the Guyanese predicament is not unique in South America. Therefore, evolution of a dominant one party government, with a very strong executive, is no surprise in view of current developments elsewhere on the Continent.

In 1964, the problems of British Guiana were violence and racial disharmony. Since that time Guyana has enjoyed a welcome measure of internal peace, but racial friction is quiescent and not dead. Credit for the peace goes to both the good sense of the Guyanese people and the leadership of Forbes Burnham. Similarly, to a great extent, the future will depend upon his wisdom and skill, or lack of it, in controlling his political party so that the people of Guyana may truly gain the unity implied in the national motto:

"One People, One Nation, One Destiny."

GUYANA

BLACK POWER?

Yereth Knowles

One major development has been the growth of black conscious-
ness and of mass economic discontent. To this already explosive
situation, we find that abuse of the political process has created a
new elite, black in hue only, dedicated to the ultimately
irreconcilable objectives of self aggrandisement and mass
leadership.[1]

Caribbean leaders have been faced with problems of political
stability for many years. The same political leaders, who themselves
in the past have espoused Marxist and/or Socialist anti-colonialist
philosophies, are now confronted with political agitation, with the
language "revolution," and some violence most often in the name of
Black Power. The enemy of Black Power today is not (directly) the
outside colonial power. The enemy is the regime, those who hold
power, political leaders who are themselves black, the same political
leaders who responded to the spontaneous protest outbursts of the
Thirties. The recent agitation (since 1967), similar to that of the
Thirties, has spread from island to island, has been spontaneous,
without a central locus of directed, organized power or persuasion—
first, Guadeloupe, Bermuda, Jamaica, and then Anguilla and Curaçao,
ending in the most dramatic mutiny in Trinidad in 1970.

Every branch of the University of the West Indies has had its share
of restlessness and of crisis, some more extreme than others. The
measure of agitation does not seem to have any relationship to
economic development or GNP of the country. Between 1962 and
1964 Guyana, a country with a per capita income of $327 (U.S.) per

---

1. Miles Fitzpatrick, *Tapia*, Election Supplement (Tunapuna, Trinidad: January 31, 1971), p. 3.

annum, was close to racial civil war, the Black West Indians versus the East Indians. Economically at the other extreme, the U.S. Virgin Islands and Bahamas with $1200 per capita income had a large share of Black Power agitation.

An outsider to these countries cannot help but feel the irony, the contradictory significance that in countries predominantly black, that is, where leaders are themselves black, inroads from the American Black Power movement have been so marked. The Black Power development has not been as accelerated in Guyana as in other parts of the Caribbean, although the pressure is now forcing radical political change. The Black Power slogan has been adopted in the English, Dutch and American areas of the Caribbean. Although there is some racial mixture of population, particularly in Trinidad and Guyana, the political actors of significance are "black" West Indians. It would be short sighted to pass off this seemingly illogical situation as a passing phase of small importance in the Caribbean, especially because of the "mutiny" in Trinidad which was close to success.[2] Black Power is a movement to be reckoned with and understood in its context. Although it stems from borrowed rhetoric of the black American Revolution, including Afros, sunglasses and dashikis, Black Power in the Caribbean has its own distinctive style, its own motives, and the genuine belief that a basic change of the system is necessary.[3]

To the leadership in the West Indies, the Black Power movement belongs to the Caribbean, as many of the crucial leadership roles in the United States were played by West Indians,[4] including Marcus Garvey, a Jamaican; Stokely Carmichael, a Trinidadian; and Rap Brown, a Jamaican. The movement is claimed as a "West Indian re-importation." In the Caribbean, leadership of many factions includes persons who have worked or studied in the United States, Canada or Great Britain. Where populations are mixed, and where

---

2. The April 1970 army uprising was significant because in one of the more advanced West Indian countries, where there had been a semblance of political stability and economic growth, a mutinous army with the assistance of "black people" took over the Government. Only the Port-of-Spain police force, the Coast Guard, and the restrictive road through the mountains were able to force the rebels to disperse and lose unified entry into Port-of-Spain. It remains unclear what the ramifications of the nearly successful government might have been.

3. *New York Times*, April 24, 1970.

4. At least they were *born* in the West Indies.

there are large numbers of East Indians (as in Trinidad), there has been an attempt to find alliances with "our black Indian brothers." This aspect has been slower in Guyana where the vestigial animosities of the Jagan-Burnham racial disputes still exist below the surface.[5] The African Society for Cultural Relations With Independent Africa, a Black Power organization, has, from time to time, reflected Burnham's party affiliation.

In Caribbean history there is little to indicate that the West Indian peoples had any grandiose illusions that independence or nationhood would quickly resolve their multiplicity of problems.[6] This is not to diminish the fact that ardent demands for constitutional reforms existed and that colonial domination was opposed; it is rather to say that the advent of nationhood was neither hurried nor considered a panacea. From personal impressions garnered in Trinidad, Grenada, and Guyana, and from a survey of the literature of the movement, it is apparent that the Black Power movement is a youth movement expressing current dissatisfaction with "things-as-they-are", both politically and economically. Despite some impressive economic development and a rapid increase of tourism (and perhaps because of it), the Caribbean states are suffering a continual crisis. The industrial and tourist development has been promoted with the firm resolve to meet the rising crisis in employment.[7] The problems stem from inadequate natural resources, from traditional single crop or mining economies, from dependency on outside powers, and from subjection to the erratic fluctuations of the world market. Added to these traditional woes is the skewered distribution of wealth. Foreign investors still control most of the natural resources including oil products, tourism, sugar, and bauxite in Guyana and Jamaica. In many areas local businesses are controlled not by the majority people, the black West Indians, but by whites, Chinese, East Indians, Jews, Portuguese and Syrians. In a sense Black Power is a movement of haves and have-nots, of local control versus "foreign" control. Newly independent states, it has been discovered, do not necessarily make for independent peoples.

5. Trinidad: 33% East Indian, 43% Blacks; Guyana: 53% East Indian, 30% Blacks, with a mixture of Chinese, Portuguese, Syrians, etc.

6. Yereth Knowles, "Caribbean Regional Cooperation," *Pacific Historian,* Vol. 14, no. 2 Spring 1970, pp. 53-54.

7. *Ibid.*

In Guyana the movement has been critical but not as venemously anti-government as in Trinidad; yet there is evidence that it has pressured the Government to move more rapidly toward a goal of nationalization of resources and industry than it might have otherwise. The cause of hostility of the young toward the present leadership in all the Caribbean countries has been disappointment with the results of economic growth, and the slowness with which the governments have altered their policies toward foreign investment and are seeking to resolve their major problems. Part of the disenchantment is with the "incentives programs" and tax holidays given to lure foreign investment to countries in desperate need of investment capital.

The Governments of the new independent states of Guyana (1966), Barbados (1966), Jamaica and Trinidad (1962) have had formidable problems to face. The leaders have sought standard economic answers to the problems of population explosion (3% per annum), unemployment, and economic dependence on outside countries. The statistics themselves show ample cause for unrest. In Jamaica the official rate of unemployment is 20%.[8] It is significant that young persons between the ages of seventeen and twenty-five years old are 30% unemployed. The statistics for unemployment in Trinidad and Guyana are similar. The fact that young persons, more educated and literate than in the past, have not had jobs and have little hopes for jobs has made an important impact on the Black Power movement. Not only is youth restless, unemployed, and hungry, but it is unprepared to sit-out the period of economic development.

It is felt bitterly by many that the economics of the countries are forcing the governments to seek foreign capital at the expense of their own independence. Colonial export economies traditionally based upon primary products are not very different from pre-independence days: sugar, petroleum, bauxite. The companies that control these products control the nation-state. Bookers in Guyana, Tate and Lyle in Trinidad, for example, still dominate sugar production. Banks and insurance companies are Canadian controlled. Bauxite is controlled by Alcoa, Kaiser, Reynolds, and Alcan (U. S.

---

8. Government Bulletin, 1969; also "Labor Law in Jamaica," U. S. Bureau of Labor Statistics Bulletin, Washington, D. C., 1969.

and Canadian) and petroleum is controlled by Texaco, Shell, B.P., and Standard Oil Company in Trinidad and Curacao. A Jamaican and Guyanese complaint is that the refining process for bauxite is accomplished outside the country, and therefore is of little benefit to the people of Guyana.[9]

There is little doubt that the leaders of today's governments in the West Indies are aware of the nature of their economic problems. These problems, if not insurmountable in face of the demands of the people, are at least horrendous. In using standard economic solutions, the politicians-economists have sought capital from outside sources in order to meet the needs of development and unemployment. Dr. Eric Williams, scholar and author of several serious books; Forbes Burnham, lawyer; and Errol Barrow, past labor leader—these men of considerable achievement and ability cannot be happy with the fact that their economies are controlled by the former colonial powers, from whom they recently won independence. Yet they see no choice in their economic policies. Following Puerto Rico's example of "Operation Bootstrap," incentive for capital and tax holiday had reached a competitive pitch (until hopefully resolved through a recent CARIFTA agreement). Overseas companies were invited into the countries to help exploit natural resources (Guyana and Jamaica in bauxite and Trinidad in oil). At the time it seemed to the leaders the method to present an immediate useful action to create economic growth. Yet to the Black Power groups now who include the seventeen to twenty-five year olds, it is called a "give away program" of national wealth.[10]

Government officials are accused of creating "a nation of servants," a "prostitution of our people" where tourism has been encouraged. Errol Barrow was quoted to the author in Barbados as answering these changes with the blunt statement that "abuse these tourists, send them home, and you will go hungry." In other words the choices are not happy choices. Young people are not willing to choose between the evils of living in substandard conditions, continually growing slums, and absence of job prospects.

William Demas, Secretary General of the Commonwealth Caribbean Secretariat indicated in a speech that though the literacy rate has been improved, school is irrelevant and does not equip the

9. Negotiations for more control of bauxite were in process in Guyana in January, 1971.
10. *New York Times.*

student vocationally. Capital intensive industry does not help the labor surplus, and luxury tourism has the effect of creating modern sector enclaves of "high paying pleasanter jobs" in an agricultural rustic environment. The lure accelerates the movement from agriculture to urban sector, which is "a double edged sword." Caribbean economies are distorted and irrational, he says, a "mixture of historical, institutional and economic factors" which distorts the patterns of incomes. There is a lack of overall unemployment strategy (or use of incomes strategy). Political stability requires the need to develop the rural sector, or what he calls agro-industry plus incomes policies—a new educational system relevant to problems.[11]

Forbes Burnham in Guyana came to power after particularly difficult times, that is after racial strife in 1964. His supporters were loyal Black West Indians in a racially divided country. The charge of "afro-saxonism" has not been as ardent against him as it has been against Eric Williams in Trinidad. Yet there seems to be some reason to believe that the move toward a Cooperative Republic in Guyana is a means of coming to terms with the anguish of the Black Power movement. The Government of Guyana, through its official bulletins and speeches, is against further foreign domination of the country's resources, is moving toward nationalization, is disarming the Marxist Jagan opposition by "out-socializing" them in the Cooperative Republic concept. In Guyana, numerous young persons claim that Burnham's program today is Jagan's program of yesterday, simply implemented at a slower pace.[12]

As the majority of the Guyanese population is East Indian (53%) and still growing, a recent Burnham political maneuver has been to include East Indians in his appointments to important government positions.[13] On the one side Burnham has had to face the political PPP-Jagan challenge, while on the other he has faced criticism from young intellectuals who have criticized his economic policies, his connection with the United States, Canada, and Great Britain, and his alleged past "CIA" taint. In 1970, on the anniversary day of the 1763 slave uprising against the Dutch, slave leader "Cuffy" was elevated to the position of national hero. Simultaneously, in a

11. Caribbean Conference, 6th Meeting, August, 1970.

12. Numerous persons echoed this point of view in January, 1971 visit of author to Georgetown.

13. Including Cheddi Jagan's brother, Derek, Deputy Speaker of the House.

symbolic act, Burnham announced the creation of the Cooperative Republic. The cooperative concept is a new effort for seeking a solution within the traditions and social milieu of the country, that is, of a cooperative participatory ownership.[14]

In Burnham's view of the Cooperative Republic, the people of Guyana will have an opportunity to actively participate in the economics of their own country. The foreign companies will be forced to share the exploited resources with the citizens of Guyana. The "self-help" program of the Cooperative Republic has the propagandistic flavor and appeal of Israel's Kibbutz program. The present moves are toward nationalization of mining and industry, yet it must be remembered that Burnham's initial power was the result of a maneuver by the British Government, with United States backing, to unseat Jagan through a coalition government (based upon proportional representation). Burnham's problems still keep him on a tightrope. Capital is necessary for development, and there is little capital within the country. The young intellectuals are demanding increased public ownership. Yet, just how much will the bauxite companies compromise in the attempt at further socialization? At what point will they regard losses greater than profit, and pull out? Will the Black Power movement press for rapid and complete confiscation?

The many problems are increasing in dimension because of the continued polarization between the incomed class and the un-employed. Dissatisfactions are channeled against the present government leadership. The proposal of a Cooperative Republic is Burnham's answer to the charge of foreign white domination or resources. He proposes Guyanese ownership of industry and commerce, farming and bauxite mining. It is not to be total ownership, but rather a profit-sharing scheme. Further, he insists that regional integration of the Caribbean countries is the only way to free the area from neo-colonial control. He has also offered Guyana's untouched interior to other, overpopulated West Indian areas for development and living.[15]

In a *New York Times* interview, Burnham discussed his move to

14. Government bulletins on the Cooperative Republic, Co-op Republic, Guyana, Georgetown, Guyana, 1970.

15. Or perhaps he wants increased black population to offset the East Indian potential domination of Guyana.

gain majority control in the Guyanese bauxite mining operation of Reynolds Metal Company and Alcan. He explained his concept of accepting "the government as trustees for the people of Guyana." "The demand for majority control by Guyana," he said, was "non-negotiable." Insisting that the Government is strong enough to fight the aluminum companies, he said:

> People tell me that a corporation like Alcan can break me, but I say it is better to be broken by a corporation like Alcan than it is to be broken by *your own people.* The alternative is to continue to be poor, to continue to be mendicants, continue to be recipients of handouts, which is the most dehumanizing experience.[16]

At times Burnham has been labeled a Black Power exponent by his opponents. His answer may lie in his own analysis of where he wishes to be placed on the historical record. By constantly facing the balance of West Indian versus East Indian power, and young intellectuals favoring the socialist cause, he may have found an answer for his own immediate future. Yet the question remains, regardless of whether this is a sincere attempt to find an answer or a political ploy, whether Guyana can develop without outside capital; whether she will stagnate; whether the companies are willing to play the game, and be "understanding," within the realm of limited profits; and whether the Government of Guyana with its lingering racial tensions, its alleged overt corruption and its inadequacy of manpower skills, can withstand its own compromise with the pressures of Black Power. A second question for Burnham: Is there any other alternative?

February 1971

16. *New York Times*, January 11, 1971 (Author's emphasis).

GUYANA

ECONOMIC DEVELOPMENT
SINCE INDEPENDENCE

Ved P. Duggal

Size and Economic Development

Guyana is a small economy and a small nation.[1] Can such a nation develop in the same way as the big and medium-sized nations have developed?

Modern economic growth of big and small nations does have many common features: a shift from agriculture to other sectors in the economy, a shift of population from rural urban areas, a shift from small-scale to large-scale enterprise; capital formation constitutes an increasing proportion of national product. The size of a country does not seem to play a large role in economic development.[2] Yet, according to Simon Kuznets, although size in and of itself is not so important, it has some effect: (a) economic structure of a small nation will be less diversified than that of a larger unit, owing to its small territory and availability of few resources, or to a small population and comparably small market; (b) at a given level of

---

1. In 1966, the year of its independence, Guyana had a per capita gross domestic product (GDP) at factor cost, and in current prices, of 515 Guyanese dollars. (G$– a Guyanese dollar is equal to U.S. $0.50, at present). The unemployed as a percentage of labor force were about 21%. (This was an official figure based on the Labor Force Survey of 1965). Population was growing at a rate of over 3% per annum, while the economy was growing at about the same rate in constant prices. Net factor income paid abroad (consisting mostly of the profits of foreign-owned companies in Guyana) was above 9% of the GDP at factor cost. More than 53% of the GDP was being generated by sugar, mining and quarrying (mostly composed of bauxite), distribution, and government sectors.

2. Amongst the big countries (China, India, U.S.S.R., U.S.A.) we have both relatively developed and underdeveloped economies; amongst the middle-sized countries (U.K., Germany, Pakistan, Indonesia, Egypt), and among small countries (Swedan, Switzerland, Ceylon, Haiti, Guyana) also we have relatively developed and underdeveloped countries.

per capita income, small nations will have more disparity between their structure of final demand and the structure of domestic product as compared with the large nations; (c) consequently the share of foreign trade in total output is greater for a small country than for a large one; (d) small nations may export few commodities to few countries, and import their requirements from these few countries; (e) foreign trade may help the small countries in overcoming the lack of diversification of production at home, but it may not be free and reliable at all times; (f) accordingly small nations may desire to pursue certain economic activities at home even though it may be inefficient to do so as economies of large-scale production are not available.[3]

Small size may have certain advantages in that consensus may be rather easily achieved as to policies regarding land tenure, control of business enterprises, taxation, foreign exchange control, since a small nation may have fewer regional, racial and other diversities. Small nations may also be relatively more flexible in decision making. This could help them in adjusting to changing technology and changing international economic relations.[4] Nonetheless, some of the small underdeveloped nations like Guyana, Ceylon, and Malaya have racial problems and for that matter have more dissentions than consensus.

Measurement of Economic Development

Before attempting to measure the economic development of Guyana, let us see what yardsticks are available to make such a measurement. The measurement of economic development of a country is not an easy job. If economic development is measured by looking at the increase in per capita product, it is possible that in the short run a country which is investing in consumer goods industries would be developing at a faster rate as compared with a country which is investing in producer goods industries. However, other things being equal, investment in producer goods industries pays off late but substantially, while investment in consumer goods industries pays off soon but not so substantially. Therefore, any use of growth

3. Simon Kuznets, *Six Lectures on Economic Growth* (New York: The Free Press, 1959), pp. 89-100.
4. *Ibid.*

in product, per capita, as an indicator of the development of a country, should also specify in what economic sector investments are being made.

Investments may also be made in the development of human potentital in a country. These investments also pay off after a relatively longer period of time. Sometimes, under the stress and strains of a situation in a country, without any visible investments, human attitudes may change so radically that rapid economic development is favored by its peoples. This change may bring about a faster rate of growth in a relatively short period. Unfortunately, a change in human attitudes, as a factor contributing to economic development, cannot be easily measured.

Certain changes in the structures or foundations of a society, and in its relations with the outside world, may greatly influence the rate of its economic development. Here also it is difficult to pinpoint quantitatively those changes in society that would result in any given rate of economic development. Qualitatively, it may be said that certain configurations of societies and attitudes, in certain historical and technological contexts, have resulted in sudden breakthroughs from relatively stagnant economic situations. In Europe, industrial revolution was made possible by the accumulations of capital and knowledge and by changes in societies and attitudes over a long stretch of time. Similarly, rapid industrialization in recent times in the communist countries is perhaps due to the borrowing of technology and changing of attitudes and social and international relations, by those countries.

Economic development cannot be achieved in a purely mechanical fashion, e.g. merely by mobilizing savings and investing them. It must be accompanied by significant changes in social and international relations, and in popular attitudes.

The difficulties in measuring economic growth, supply of empirical data apart, lie precisely in this point: modern economic growth implies major structural changes and correspondingly large modifications in social and institutional conditions under which the greatly increased product per capita is attained.[5]

5. Kuznets, p. 15

Nonetheless in order to measure economic development the changing elements of the structure must be reduced to a common denominator. This common denominator is the rate of growth of per capita product. Other indicators of development may be: the rate of increase in productivity, increasing contribution made by manufacturing sector to G.D.P., change in the size of the base of the economy (in the sense of diversification), balance of payments situation, employment situation, implementation of development programs, and, perhaps, increase in retail trade, registration of motor vehicles, and electricity production.

Economic Development of Guyana Since Independence[6]

(a) *The rate of growth of per capita product*

The average rate of growth of per capita G.D.P. (at factor cost) in current prices has been about 3.5% per year between 1960 and 1969, and about 5.7% per year between 1966 and 1969. In constant prices of 1960, it has been about 1% between 1960 and 1969, while between 1960 and 1965 it was almost nil. At prices of 1966, it has been 3.1% between 1966 and 1969.[7]

The average rate of increase of population since 1966 comes to about 2.7% per year, while an unofficial source puts it at over 3%. Similarly, there has been an average per year increase in prices, since 1966, of 2.4% while the same unofficial source puts it at about 4%.[8] Therefore, according to the unofficial source, the average rate of growth of per capita G.D.P. since 1966, in constant prices, would come to about 1% per year. The rate of growth of per capita product according to statistics given in the Bank of Guyana *Annual Report* for 1967 would come to −1% for 1966 and 1967, if one were to concede the average per year increase in prices and population of 4% and 3%, respectively.

6. The reader should remember that the following analyses and conclusions are based on a very limited time span, 1966-1970.

7. Official figures are drawn from the *Guyana Consumer Index* (GDP) and the Bank of Guyana, *Annual Report, 1969* (population). Unofficial source is: Cheddi Jagan, *For a United Free Guyana*, mimeographed, 1968, 1969, pp. 15, ff.

8. Cheddi Jagan, *For a Unified Guyana* (1968, 1969) (mimeographed), p. 15

On the whole, real income growth has scarcely kept up with population growth since independence or even since 1960.[9] According to British Guiana (Guyana) Development Programme (1966-1972) the same was the case between 1954 and 1960.[10] It seems that "the economy of Guyana has an underlying tendency to stagnate" due to its basic structural and institutional weaknesses.[11]

(b) *The rate of increase in productivity*

The rate of increase in productivity (i.e. G.D.P./Labor force), as an indicator of economic development, has been meager. The ratio of G.D.P. to total labor force was about G$1700 in 1965, G$1652 in 1966, G$1663 in 1967, G$1660 in 1968, and G$1666 in 1969.[12]

(c) *Composition of G.D.P. by product* (Table 1)

Over the last decade contributions to G.D.P. of mining and quarrying and government have gone up, while that of sugar and rice have gone down. The shares of livestock, fishing, and forestry in the generation of G.D.P., have not changed substantially. Guyana, with a large area, a reasonably long sea coast, and huge forests, could put a

9. *Cf.* "The past decade or so witnessed an annual growth rate in terms of Gross Domestic Product of around 4-5 per cent per annum. When this is deflated for price increases, the real annual increase in G.D.P. was between 3-4 per cent. Since population was increasing at about the same rate as real gross domestic product incomes per head remained almost static or showed very slight increases." Wilfred L. David, *Economic Problems of Guyana Today in Caribbean Development and the Future of the Church* (Proceedings of a conference held in Georgetown, Guyana, 1969).

10. British Guiana, Government Printery, *Development Programme. 1966-1972* (Georgetown, British Guiana [Guyana]), pp. 1-2.

11. L. Best. *Economic Planning in Guyana, in the Caribbean in Transition* (Rio Piedras: UPR, Institute of Caribbean Studies, 1965), p. 60.

12. Calculated from the statistics in the Bank of Guyana Annual Report, 1969. If, according to standard accounting practice, depreciation, imports and the service on foreign debt were deducted from the GDP, the ratio of GDP to labor force would be lower still. It might even affect the rate of increase in productivity as defined above, depending on depreciation, imports and the service on foreign debt in different years. Unfortunately, figures about depreciation in different years are not available. Therefore, standard social accounting practice could not be observed. Instead of taking employed force as a denominator in the above mentioned ratio, total labor force figures were used because an important part of development planning is to provide jobs to the unempoyed. Benjamin Higgins, *Economic Development, Principles, Problems, and Policies* (London: Constable and Co., LTD., 1959), pp. 630-635.

TABLE 1

PERCENTAGE DISTRIBUTION OF GUYANESE G.D.P. (At Factor Cost)

	1960	1961	1962	1963	1964	1965	1966	1967	1968	1969
Sugar	17.5	17.2	16.9	25.2	14.6	14.5	12.3	13.8	12.4	13.4
Rice	5.2	5.4	4.9	4.7	6.7	6.2	5.6	4.2	4.1	3.1
Livestock	1.2	2.3	3.1	2.5	2.7	2.5	2.1	2.2	2.2	2.2
Other Agriculture	3.3	3.1	3.1	2.6	2.7	2.8	2.8	2.8	2.8	2.9
Fishing	1.5	2.0	2.0	2.1	2.1	2.3	2.5	2.4	2.0	1.5
Forestry	2.5	2.3	2.0	1.5	1.6	1.5	1.9	1.4	1.5	2.0
Mining & Quarrying	11.0	12.8	16.2	12.9	17.6	16.4	16.9	17.5	19.5	20.4
Food & Tobacco	2.1	2.2	2.3	3.0	3.6	3.8	3.8	3.8	3.8	3.8
Other Mfg.	3.1	2.8	3.0	2.8	2.9	3.6	3.6	3.7	4.0	3.8
Distribution	14.1	13.5	11.9	13.3	12.9	12.0	12.1	11.8	11.1	10.6
Tpt. & Communic.	7.5	7.5	6.5	6.5	6.5	6.4	6.8	6.4	6.5	6.3
Eng. and Const.	9.4	7.1	6.7	5.0	4.9	5.2	6.2	6.6	7.4	7.7
Rent of Dwellings	3.1	2.8	2.7	3.1	2.7	2.5	2.5	2.5	2.4	2.2
Financial Services	3.2	3.1	3.0	3.1	2.9	2.9	3.1	3.0	2.9	2.7
Other Services	4.9	4.5	4.4	4.4	4.4	4.2	4.3	4.1	3.9	3.6
Government	9.7	10.5	9.9	10.2	10.8	12.2	12.5	13.2	12.7	12.9

Source: Bank of Guyana Annual Report for 1969, p. 90.

lot of hope for future growth on livestock, fishing and forestry. The contribution of manufacturing has remained steady, although the seven-year development plan of Guyana initiated in 1966, and inspired by the Puerto Rican model of development, emphasized the attracting of foreign capital for the manufacturing sector.[13]

(d) *Change in the size of the base of the economy* (Table 1)

The G.D.P. is attributable in large part to but a few industries. Sugar, bauxite, distribution and government, have contributed more than 50% to G.D.P.; twelve other industries have contributed the remainder.

13. To attract and hold private-enterprise the government did what the plan had asked it to do, namely, it provided good and efficient transport and communication systems, and gave full scope to personal initiative in agriculture, in industry, in trade, in commerce, in construction and finance. The share of agriculture in development expenditure went down during 1965-1969, while that of transportation, communications and roads went up. Full scope to private enterprise was provided through increased development expenditures on public works and through credits to private businesses. *British Guiana (Guyana) Development Programme, 1966-1972*, pp. 1-5; Bank of Guyana, *Annual Report, 1967*, p. 76.

(e) *Balance of payments situation* (Table 2)

Since 1965 the balance of payments has been in deficit. That deficit has been largely caused by the great outflow of income according to foreign investments as indicated by the imports of services in Table 2.

(f) *Increase in employment*

Unemployment, as percentage of labor force, was 10.8 in 1960 and 14.1 in 1965.[14] According to the (British) Guyana Development Program the level of unemployment for March 1965 was 20.9%.[15]

(g) *Implementation of development program*

According to a confidential progress report of the Government of Guyana the implementation of the program during 1966-1968 was

14. These figures are from the Bank of Guyana, *Annual Report, 1969.*

BANK OF GUYANA AND BRITISH GUIANA (GUYANA) DEVELOPMENT PROGRAMME (1966-1972) FIGURES ABOUT EMPLOYMENT, UNEMPLOYMENT AND UNDEREMPLOYMENT (THOUSANDS)

Period	Labor Force		Labor Force as % of population of 14 and over		Employed	
	BOG	D.P.	BOG	D.P.	BOG	D.P.
1956	...	164.6	...	69.6	...	135.0
1960	175.0	...	58.1	...	156.1	...
1965	193.1	174.6	60.6	54.9	165.9	138.1

Table—Continued

Employed as % of Labor Force		Unemployed		Unemployed as % of Labor Force	
BOG	D.P.	BOG	D.P.	BOG	D.P.
...	57.1	...	29.6	...	18.0
89.2	...	18.8	...	10.8	...
85.9	43.4	27.2	36.4	14.1	20.9

BOG—Bank of Guyana
D.P.—British Guiana (Guyana) Development Programme

15. Jagan, p. 12. Official figures are not available for 1969 but unofficially it may be said that the employed as a percentage of labor force are less than before.

TABLE 2

BALANCE OF PAYMENTS

GS Million	1962	1963	1964	1965	1966	1967	1968[1]	1969[1]
Exports of Goods f.o.b.	164	176	169	177	192	218	235	250
Imports of Goods, c.i.f.	−126	−119	−151	−181	−202	−226	−220	−238
Balance of Goods	38	57	18	− 4	− 10	− 8	15	12
Export of Services	28	20	25	29	28	30	31	33
Imports	− 63	− 51	− 60	− 62	− 68	− 72	− 72	− 80
Balance of Goods and Services	3	26	− 17	− 37	− 50	− 50	− 26	− 35
Net Capital Inflow[2]	8	− 13	25	24	38	64	24	26
Change in Net Foreign Assets of Banking System (Increase "−")	− 1	− 13	− 8	13	12	− 14	2	9

[1] The figures for visibles, invisibles and capital inflow for 1968 revised, but not final estimates. The corresponding estimates for 1969 are first approximations.

[2] Net inflow of funds from abroad, including grants.

Source: Bank of Guyana Annual Report for 1967, p. 15.

retarded. The program envisaged an average annual expenditure of about G$43 million, but the average actual expenditures per year was only G$34 million.

(h) *Increase in retail trade, new registration of motor vehicles, electricity production, etc.*

The retail trade has increased from G$138 per person in 1966 to G$142 in 1968, an increase of a mere G$4. The number of persons per newly-registered motor vehicle has gone up, from 130 in 1966 to 165 in 1969. The electricity production per person increased from 326 Kwh in 1966 to 390 Kwh in 1969.[16] Much of that increase in electricity production apparently has been caused by the bauxite and industry expansion during that period.

Reasons for Lack of Development

The slow development of Guyana cannot be attributed to a low level of capital formation. The ratio of investment, both public and

16. All the statistics calculated from Bank of Guyana, *Annual Report, 1969*.

private, to G.D.P. for the period 1966 to 1969 was 26%. This is a high ratio by international standards. Lack of development in Guyana may be caused by certain fundamental characteristics of the economy.

(a) Guyana's Economic Dependence on the Outside World

The economy of Guyana relies heavily on foreign trade: ratio of exports to G.D.P. in 1969 was 57% and ratio of imports to G.D.P. was 54%.[17] Foreign trade may not be very advantageous for a country like Guyana whose bargaining power is weak. In a free market, terms of trade have been found to be generally unfavorable to countries exporting raw materials and agricultural products. The manufacturing sector (which includes the processing of agricultural crops, but excludes the processing of minerals) in Guyana makes a very small contribution to G.D.P. Any increase in import prices relative to export prices may sharply affect investment and wages.

Total domestic capital formation is financed heavily by foreign resources—about 35% in 1960. Foreign banks in Guyana also finance consumer credit and thus siphon off household savings. Hire-purchase credit for motor cars and consumer durables was 64% of total credit outstanding in August 1969. All this has resulted in the dependence of the economy on foreign capital. Historically, foreign capital has owned the most profitable sectors of production, such as sugar and bauxite.[18] It has also dominated the foreign and wholesale trade, banking, insurance and shipping. Net factor income paid abroad is a relatively large share of G.D.P., i.e., about 9% on the average between 1960 and 1969.[19]

In brief the economy of Guyana is geared to overseas markets.

17. Different commodity groups as a percentage of total imports were as follows, in 1969: Consumer Goods 28.56%, producer good 43.42%, intermediate goods, 28.01%. And different commodity groups as a percentage of total export were as follows in 1969: sugar 36.39%, ores 38.51%, rice 8.37%.

18. Sugar, bauxite and alumina (a product of bauxite) account for 72% of Guyanese exports by value.

19. This is an important share of the GDP. For example, it can increase investment by almost 33%. Compare it with the following: In 1949, repatriated profits of foreign firms, in percentage of the national income, were 4% in South Africa, 4% in Southern Rhodesia, 5% in Surinam, 6% in Santo Domingo, and 13% in Iran. Cf. U.N.O., *National Income and Its Distribution in Underdeveloped Countries*, Statistical Papers, Series E (New York, 1951), p. 10.

Exchange control, which existed for some years during the previous regime, was abolished in 1965. Import licensing is not practiced. The supply of money and domestic price level are dependent on autonomous actions of foreign banks, which are independent of balance of payments situation, and of movements in export and import prices.

Foreign aid is granted but with strings attached. Minister of Finance Dr. P. Reid in his 1968 budget statement said:

> But though foreign aid is welcomed Guyana cannot accept aid under any conditions; hence unfortunately aid from some donor countries has not been fully utilized during the year under review[1967].

The tied funds increase the project costs unduly because imports cannot be bought from the cheapest sources. Moreover, some aid donors want to charge a relatively high rate of interest.

> All of these factors together with the requirement of the aid donors that pre-loan studies by independent agencies approved by the aid donor be carried out and that the project itself be watched over by high-priced consultants only make for a high-priced project. There is no other area in which the methods of operations of the aid donors act as a limitation to growth. Reference must be made to the fact that because of the shortage of local funds high priority projects can only be financed by approaches to the aid donors which projects may not be attractive to such donors; the upshot is that in quest for development finance projects of lower priority are selected, financed and implemented.[20]

The situation of dependence is apparently so complete that the attitudes of the people to government, structures of business organization, and habits of consumption, saving and investment behavior are derived from the "modern" countries.

(b) *Lack of Integration in the Economy*

The economy of Guyana relies too heavily on the highly capital-intensive sugar cane- and bauxite-oriented industries. For

20. *Development Program Progress Report, 1966-1968*, (Report to Second Aid Donors Conference), p. 2.

their capital and management they depend on foreign countries. In 1960, those industries contributed 26% to G.D.P. but provided only 14% of total jobs.

The sugar industry can sustain the economy at a long run rate of growth of income equal to population growth, only if there is a continuing increase in its prices. This is so because the industry is not a basic one, i.e., it has few backward and forward linkages to augment sugar-based and sugar-oriented industries. Moreover, export of sugar is dependent on special preferences granted mainly by the United Kingdom. How long the United Kingdom can continue to do so in view of the low price of Cuban sugar and the weakness of its own economy is a moot question.[21]

The bauxite industry does have both forward and backward links. However, the forward links depend on the availability of capital and technology to expand bauxite-based industries. The backward links consist in earning of revenues and foreign exchange through the exportation of bauxite and allocation of these resources to economic development. The revenues and foreign exchange from the export sector can be increased only if there is an expansion in the output of export goods, or an increase in their prices, or an increase in the national share of foreign earnings, or a combination thereof.

There is a dualism within the agriculture sector. The sugar cane plantations produce crops with a rather high capital-intensive technology, for export to foreign markets. On the other hand, small rice farms produce with a rather low capital-intensive technology for domestic as well as export markets. There is a genuine lack of credit facilities available to small farmers. On the whole, as in the industry sector, there is a lack of diversification in agriculture.

Agriculture, manufacturing and infra-structure are not developing in a balanced, proportionate fashion. Agricultural production cannot be increased because there is a shortage of reclaimed land. Most of the reclaimed fertile land near the coast is used for sugar plantations.

---

21. "Sugar production is not based on the dynamic components of either internal or world demand. Its products are essentially limited (sugar, rum and molasses). The utilization of wastes in the industry (e.g., the use of sugar tops as fodder) has not been adequate. In some of the alternative land uses, e.g., livestock, the situation is different. It can, for example, include animal feeds, fresh meats, dairy products, the vast potted and preserved meat industry, hides, leather and leather products. (A small country like Israel already has over 5000 employed in the leather products industry alone)." Clive Thomas, *Sugar Economics in a Colonial Situation*, p. 55.

In order to reclaim new land, much investment is required. Aluminum smelting has not been undertaken, nor has much other manufacturing yet been started.[22] The development of infrastructure, such as technical and other educational institutions, communications and utilities, requires both a public administration tuned to the purpose and a higher rate of taxation. Yet taxation of company income, a major source of revenues in many countries, yields little revenue owing to the tax holidays allowed to the companies. Further, because of a rather slow development of the manufacturing sector, not many new enterprises have been undertaken recently.

There is an overall lack of integration between monetary and fiscal matters, foreign corporations, labor unions, and foreign sector in general. This too hinders the economic development of Guyana.

(c) *Labor and Economic Development*

A rapid increase in wages may affect employment, capital formation, and government budget adversely. In Guyana there is strong trade unionism in big corporations that induces workers to seek high wages. Labor is thus stratified into high-paid workers in big firms and low-paid workers in small firms. Workers from rural areas continue to be attracted to urban areas in search of better-paid jobs, thus worsening the employment situation.

To a great extent the Guyanese economy is dependent on the service sector, as can be seen from Table 3. Such dependence implies much underemployment and lack of opportunities for more productive employment rather than transformation of the economy.

Organized labor asks for higher wages and fringe benefits both in the more and in the less productive industries. This results in an increasing rate of unemployment through further mechanization and

22. This is the situation in spite of the fact that "Guyana with its vast areas of valuable deposits of minerals, forests, agricultural land and various raw materials is the ideal country for industrialization since it offers prosperity to many types of industrial projects.

"The rivers flow from south to north into the sea and these could be converted into most of the economical transportation routes through the country.

"Guyana is well situated between the North and South American continents and could become the bridge for the highly developed North and the rapidly progressing South and so offer impressive opportunities as the North was offering before one century ago." O. V. Vrany, *Industry (in) Guyana* (Guyana Development Corporation, 1969), Introduction.

TABLE 3

EMPLOYMENT BY SECTORS, 1960 (PERCENTAGES)

Agriculture	37.0
Mining and Quarrying	3.8
Manufacturing (including processing of Agricultural Products)	16.3
Construction	8.0
Transport and Communications	4.8
Distribution	11.3
Other Services	18.8
TOTAL	100.0

Source: William G. Demas, *The Economics of Development in Small Countries, with Special Reference to the Caribbean* (Montreal, 1965), p. 110.

automatization. There is a high growth in the labor force. This need not be alarming in view of the potential resources of Guyana. However, new investments are usually made in capital-intensive projects which are mainly intented to exploit available and not potential resources.[23]

CARIFTA

The dependence of the Guyanese economy on the rest of the world, the low degree of its integration, and its labor problems, may to a certain extent be alleviated by the formation of the Caribbean Free Trade Association (CARIFTA). One of the objectives of the CARIFTA is to encourage the balanced and progressive development of the economies of its member countries: Guyana, Trinidad & Tobago, Jamaica, Barbados, the Leeward Islands, and the Windward Islands. Its other objectives concern the expansion and diversification of trade among member countries in conditions of fair competition.

23. "Not only have the schemes of incentives to industry and tax holidays failed to attract the desired level of foreign capital, but have proved costly in the sense that the capital-employment ratio of a typical industry attracted under such conditions has been in the vicinity of $15,000 to 1 (person employed)." Wilfred L. David, "Economic Planning in Guyana: Historical Review and Evaluation" *in Caribbean Development and the Future of the Church* (Proceedings of a conference held in Georgetown, Guyana, 1969).

The achievement of those objectives in turn should help the balanced and progressive development of the economies concerned.

One scholar believes that:

the CARIFTA illustrates the determination of the existing hierarchy and particularly the entrenched business interests to maintain, support and perpetuate the irrational and artificial society which their ancestors created and kept in the West Indies over the past five hundred years. . . . CARIFTA is an instrument designed to frustrate meaningful change and to maintain in being the synthetic societies of the Caribbean.[24]

He may be right as long as the CARIFTA area, as a whole, is as dependent and unintegrated as Guyana is at present, and remains without a common external tarriff. For Guyana, CARIFTA may even be a curse in disguise: foreign enterprise, with CARIFTA allowing free movement of goods without tariff walls, would like to site its plants in low-wage, custom duty-free, and income tax-free islands rather than in Guyana. Only those foreign enterprises might be sited in Guyana which require heavy and bulky Guyanese raw materials and are capital-intensive.

24. James Millete, "The Caribbean Free Trade Association: The West Indies at the Crossroads," *NEW WORLD* 4, no. 4 (Jamaica, 1968), quoted by Gerard Latortue in "The Caribbean Free Trade Association," mimeographed (San German: InterAmerican Univ.).

GUYANA

PROBLEMS IN AMERINDIAN ACCULTURATION

Della Walker

It is a truism that all nations have social problems. However, Guyana is in the enviable position of having at least one social problem of such classical nature that she can study the great variety of solutions which have been attempted and evaluate them before she embarks upon a solution of her own.

That problem is the question of how to integrate her aboriginal population, the Amerindians, who number more than 30,000 at the present time.[1] In Guyana there are representatives of nine tribal groups, that is, people with different linguistic and historical roots. The best known outside of Guyana are the Arawaks and Caribs, both carriers of Amerindian culture to the Caribbean. Between the sixth and the eighteenth centuries the Dutch planters of the Guyanas lived in relative harmony with the Amerindians, giving them iron tools in exchange for services as guides and hunters, particularly hunters of escaped slaves. After 1814, when Guyana was ceded to the British, the Amerindians' contact with the western world expanded through contact with missionaires of the Church of England and, later, the Catholic Church. Schooling and medical attention were the rewards of conversion, and the process of acculturation was accelerated.

In the twentieth century the traditional areas of occupation and the life style of the Amerindians are changing rapidly. The forces of change are both internal and external. Internally, they include new aspirations and a new self-image brought about by education and contact with the modern world. Externally, there is a growing

1. The word Amerindians has been coined to distinguish the Indians of the Americas from their East Indian namesakes.

scarcity of animals to hunt, fish to catch, and virgin land to exploit by traditional slash-and-burn methods of cultivation. There are also new money-earning jobs available which absorb the time formerly used in food-getting pursuits. Population is increasing rapidly, thus changing traditional demography. The government is also urging better utilization of valuable forest and mineral resources in those same lands.

The anthropologist, looking at such a multiplicity of problems notes, one recurring theme: the need to know the culture as it was in order to understand the effects of the present changes. Methods to accelerate change and at the same time avoid loss of identity with one's culture requires care in planning and execution.

The Amerindians of Guyana are made up of a number of linguistic groups, and villages tend to be composed of members of one, or at most two, of those groups. The region where each linguistic group resides is fairly well established. Individual identity tends to be to a particular village rather than to some broader tribal association.

There are five distinct categories based upon the technology employed in food getting:

(1) Simple hunting, fishing and gathering;
(2) Traditional Amerindian horticulture, principally the cultivation of two types of cassava, using a simple slash-and-burn technology, supplemented by traditional fishing and hunting practices;
(3) The expansion of the food base to include the cultivation of plants introduced by the earliest European settlers, i.e. plantains, bananas, and, in some places, sugar cane;
(4) The expansion of the food base by the acquisition of cattle, introducing a new technological level, namely animal husbandry;
(5) The utilization of modern agricultural methods with European crops and domesticated animals.

The greatest number are at the third stage. Unfortunately, time is not on the side of the Amerindians and the gradual technological changes of the past are too slow to meet the population growth and material aspirations of the young. The consequences of population pressure are a reduction of hunting and fishing activities. Replacement foods from the garden and stores are predominantly starches—unsuitable substitutes, from the nutritional point of view. Studies of Amerindians in Ecuador, living under similar conditions, show that the results of that change are a high level of malnutrition, lowered resistance to disease, higher infant mortality, lowered longevity and a higher rate of still births. There are strong indications that forthcoming surveys of nutritional conditions in Guyana will substantiate these findings.

In connection with the problem of loss of protein sources, the alternatives are already well known: the cultivation of protein-rich plants or the use of domesticated animals for meat. Both of these innovations have been introduced, but neither has been widely accepted. Consideration of how they were introduced, often accompanied by pressure to abandon old beliefs, may reveal reasons for this lack of internalization. The Amerindian has as yet to utilize fully the standard practices of animal husbandry vis á vis the cattle industry. The more common pattern has been to allow cattle to run free until such time as they are needed for food or sale and then to hunt them as other game was hunted in the past. While this system may be less threatening to the old ways, its inefficiency fails to alleviate current nutritional problems.

Basic to that situation is the Amerindian attitude toward domesticated animals. There seems to be little empirical data on this point. Gerald Durrell, in a delightfully informal book, *Three Singles to Adventure,* reports his experiences in collecting wild animals in Guyana, and mentions the great number and variety of pets found in Amerindian villages.[2] One of the annual reports of the Temehri Group, an organization of professionals dedicated to finding ways of helping the Amerindian help himself, recounts the discouraging attempts to improve protein nutrition through the introduction of various domesticated animals.[3] For some reason as yet unexplained, the use of domesticated animals for food does not fit comfortably into the Amerindian world-view. Apparently, only those who have radically changed their beliefs and life style have been able to employ this solution.

The mechanism of change which results in a shift from hunting to

2. Durrell, Gerald, *Three Singles to Adventure,* Rupert Hart-Davis, London, 1954, Penguin Books, 1964, p. 146 ff.

3. Temehri Group *Annual Report,* December 31, 1967 (mimeographed publication for membership distribution) Dr. L. Chin, ed.

the use of domesticated animals is not well documented but appears to have its roots in a developmental process in which the hunter, after long periods of association, begins to concentrate on certain animals, hunting them to the exculsion of all others; he studies their habits, perfects tools especially adapted to that particular animal and develops specialized ways of cooking and preserving the meat. It is a short step from those techniques to actual domestication of the animal. Attention to the life cycle of a few animals introduces a pattern of living which closeley resembles the seasonal habits of sedentary agricultural people. A corresponding domestication of plants with a similar seasonal cycle completes the change. Few, if any of the Amerindians of Guyana were at this stage when European agriculture was introduced. They are reported to have ranged over wide areas and hunted a great variety of animals.

Ethnographic material concerning the Amerindians varies from group to group and generalizations about the Amerindians are useful principally as models. Careful detailed research, with help from the generation that was trained according to the traditional ways and has since been subjected to the modern pressures, should be attempted. That procedure would reveal details, previously overlooked, which might account for the slow change in domestication of animals in contrast tó so many other changes. For example, the cultural reintegration necessary to fit the motor and the radio into Amerinidan lives seem to have met with much less resistance.

The dysfunctional elements or stress factors are frequently revealed when studied by the comparative method, in this case by attempting to ascertain attitudes and beliefs related to a given group of ideas while moving from area to area. It would be necessary to select carefully, on the basis of all available data, the areas to be studied, since they must represent as fully as possible discreet positions along a scale based upon the categories mentioned earlier. The variable becomes the degree of acculturation. The point at which attitudes show marked change is the stress area.

With this foreknowledge, added to much more gathered in other ways, agencies responsible for policy making can hope to make decisions which result in less stress and hence better and more rapid acceptance of innovation. This is turn will speed integration and bring about the desired participation in wider Guyanese society without the scars of forced acculturation.

GUYANA

WILDLIFE AND POLLUTION

Alexander D. Acholonu

> *I never saw a more beautiful country, nor more lively prospects, hills so raised here and there over the valleys, the river winding into divers branches, the plains adjoining without bush or stubble, all fair green grass, the ground hard sand easy to march on, either for horse or foot, the deer crossing in every path, the birds toward the evening singing on every tree with a thousand different tunes, cranes and herons of white crimson and carnation perching on the river's side, the air fresh with a gentle easterly wind, and every stone that we stopped to take up promised either gold or silver by its complexion.*
>
> Sir Walter Raleigh

Land and Vegetation

The natural vegetation of any country depends on its soils and climate, and its animal life depends, in turn, on the vegetation. Guyana's vegetation is as varied as its terrain. Along the coast is a low, flat alluvial land. To the south, a hilly sand and clay land stretches almost across the entire width of the country. In the hinterland are the highlands which occupy the west and south of the country, forming natural boundaries with Venezuela and Brazil, along with savannahs with their open vistas that are considered by some as the most picturesque part of Guyana. The Rupununi Savannahs occupy the south-western portion of the country. Park-land savannahs, known as Intermediate Savannahs, occur in the white sands area of the country. Coastal savannahs are also prevalent in the eastern part of Guyana.

66

Guyana, like other South American countries is endowed with a great diversity of plants. Individuals of the same species are sparsely distributed. This diversity of species is characteristic of the tropics.

Wildlife

Guyana abounds in wildlife, as do its South American neighbors. The richness of the fauna can be, in part, accounted for by the aforementioned richness and diversity of the flora and, in part, by interaction among the animal species themselves. There seems to be a balanced plant and animal community in harmony with the physical environment.

Not surprisingly, the fauna of Guyana is similar to those of the other tropical regions of the continent. This could be attributed to the fact that the entire continent has had a similar geological history.[1]

1. It is believed that in the geological past the earth had a different face. The continental drift theory postulates that throughout the Paleozoic and most of the Mesozoic eras the presently distributed continents were grouped into two great land masses—a northern Laurasia separated from a southern Gandwana by the sea of Thethys. In the cretaceous period, the land fragmented and drifted apart. Laurasia is supposed to have split into North America, Greenland, Europe and most of Asia; Gandwana, into South America, Africa, Malagasy (Madagascar), India, Australia and Antartica. Convincing evidence of a link between South America and Africa is the jigsaw-puzzle fit of the Atlantic Coast of Africa and South America, and the close affinities of fossils, rocks and life forms of the opposite sides of the Atlantic.

There was a time, then, when South America had the same type of fauna as the rest of Gandwana. When its connection with the southern land masses was severed, the continent and its life forms stayed isolated for a very long time. During this period, some peculiar and exotic life species developed on the continent. With the establishment of a land bridge between North and South America at the isthmus of Panama. There was an influx of northern animals into South America, thus effecting a mingling of indigenous animals and migrant forms.

Some of the indigenous animals which existed before the inception of the land bridge are the lungfish (*Osteichthyes*); the Matamata, the Side-naked turtles and the boas (*Reptilia*); rhea and hoatzin (*Aves*); and the oppossums, armadillos, sloths and anteaters (*Mammalia*). The fact that the lungfish had relations in Africa and Australia, and the Surinam toad has relations in Africa, accentuates the existence of a single land-mass in the Southern Hemisphere in the geological past.

Some of the North American animals which invaded the South are the New World (or prehensile) monkeys which were among the first invaders of this continent, the deer, raccoon, cats, squirrels, bears and some others well represented in North America. Horses and cattle were imported by the first European settlers.

Herpetofauna

In Guyana amphibians and reptiles are found in abundance, since the prevailing tropical climatic conditions of damp atmosphere, swamps, and rain forests, are propitious to their existence. Several of them have camouflage characteristics. For instance, the Matamata, an unusual turtle, is difficult to tell apart from a mass of dry leaves; a caiman is often mistaken for a dry log; an anaconda, or water camudi, may be confused with a huge submerged root. Some are endowed with cryptic or protective coloration and are capable of changing their colors as they move from one background to another. These characteristics leave one who knows little about them with the erroneous impression that they are scarce in the country. Also of importance are their behavior patterns. They are not an active group and feed infrequently. Most of the amphibians and some reptiles inhabit damp and shady places in order to conserve energy.

The most common amphibians are the toads (*Bufo* spp.) which are commonly seen during the early rains and often at night. The Surinam toad (*Pipa americana*) which occurs here is, as afore-mentioned, related to species common in Africa with no close relatives in the New World. Several species of pipid and tree frogs occur in the interior. About four species are believed to serve as edibles for the Amerindians. Salamanders are lacking according to a noted Poonai.[2] That, however, is not surprising since those species are notoriously absent in most tropical areas. They are usually not heat-resistant.

Reptiles are well represented. The anolid lizards and geckos are commonly seen in residential areas, the tegu lizards of fairly large size are found mostly in farms and low woods and the teiid lizards are plentyful in sandy places. The iguanas abound especially in the coastlands and are of diverse colors and sizes. They are eaten by some people and are considered a delicacy.

Four crocodilian species are recorded in Guayana. The dwarf caiman (*Paleosuchus trigonatus*) occurs mainly in the hilly interior, in the slow-moving creeks. Another species is the smooth-fronted or upland caiman (*Paleoscichus palpebrosus*). The commonest one

2. N.O. Poonai, "Wilderness and Wildlife in Guyana," *Cooperative Republic: A Study of Aspects of Our Way of Life* (Georgetown: Guyana Lithographic Co., Ltd., 1970), p. 161-194.

found all over the country is the secretive spectacled caiman (*Caiman crocodilus*). It is, however, said to belong to the flat coastlands. This species and the black caiman (*Melanosuchus niger*), the largest of all and occuring in the swamps and rivers of the hinterland are very much hunted for their skins which are highly treasured—used for curio trade.

There are several kinds of snakes. The common boas include the water camudi or anaconda (*Eunectes murinus*), the land camudi or boa constrictor (*Constrictor constrictor*), the emerald tree boa (*Boa canina*), the rainbow boa (*Epicrates cenchria*), the gray tree boa (*Corallus enydeis*), Cook's tree boa (*Boa cooki*), and the brown tree boa (*Boa annulata*). Although some of these grow to large sizes, they are not poisonous but rather crush their prey before swallowing them. A rat snake (*Spilotes pullatus*) and the yellow tail (*Drymarchon corais*) also occur here as do several species of non-poisonous water snakes. Among the poisonous snakes are a rattlesnake (*Crotalus terrificus*), the bushmaster (*Lachesis muta*), and labaria (*Bothrops atrox*). Several species of poisonous coral snakes (*Micrurus* sp.), some with red, yellow and black bands which serve as warning to other animals, are also in the country but are rarely seen.[3]

There are three groups of turtles. The marine turtles, which include the green turtle (*Chelonia mydas*), atlantic ridley (*Lepidochelys olivared*), leather back (*Dermochelys coriacea*), and hawksbill, (*Eretmochelys imbricata*). These are often molested and taken in considerable numbers when they come ashore to lay their eggs, which are also taken. The swamp and river turtles such as (*Geomyda punctularia*), Cayenne river turtle (*Podocnemis cayennensis*), Dumeril's river turtle (*Padocnemis dumeriliana*), a side-necked turtle (*Phrynops geoffronanus*) and Arrau (*Podocnemis expansa*), a large turtle which is not only hunted but whose eggs, usually laid on the sand banks, are collected indiscriminately by people. Two species of land turtles or tortoises, (*Testudo denticulata* and *T. carbonaria*) which occur here are also hunted and eaten by some people.

Avifauna

Birds in Guyana are numerous and varied, especially the passerine species. There are over seven hundred species in this country

3. *Ibid.*

including both resident and migrant forms. Brilliant or protective coloration is an outstanding feature of most of them.

Some of the more prominent larger birds include the Crested and Harpy Eagles, the Jabiru (*Jabiru myeteria*), Maguari Storks (*Euxenura maguari*) and the Honora Crane. The Scarlet Ibis (*Eudocimus ruber*), the Chestnut-bellied Heron (*Agamia agami*), and the King Vulture (*Sarcoramphus papa*) are very colorful.

Included in the group of beautiful birds are the toucans, familiarly called bill-birds. They are noted for their grotesque and lavishly colored beaks. There are many species in the country. While the Red-billed Toucan (*Ramphastos monilis*) is the most common, the Orange-billed Toucan (*Ramphastos aurantiirostris*) is perhaps the most beautiful.

Birds of prey, such as eagles, vultures and owls, and game birds abound in Guyana. Quails, tree ducks, pigeons, parrots, guans, and teals are among the game birds shot for sport.

Among the hummingbirds present in the country are the Ruby Topaz, the Crimson Topaz, and the Tufted Coquette. The song birds include the finches, orioles, tanagers and cuphonias. These, as well as the parrots and parakeets, are commonly kept in captivity as pets. Some common cotingas, birds of the great forests, are the Umbrella Bird, the Bell Bird, and the Calf Bird.

There are some birds in Guyana which are now in the category of rare and endangered species. The Hoatzin (*Opisthocomus cristatus*), a gallinaceous bird also called Cange Pheasant in Guyana, is one of these. It is found in some Guyana rivers in swampy areas. It is of interest because of the peculiar habits displayed by its fledglings to insure protection. The young Hoatzin when in danger, dives headlong into deep water, and crawls up to its nest in a tree later when the danger has passed. The young are equipped with temporary functional claws on the wings which make quadrupedal movements among tangled vegetation possible. This is an interesting reminder of how the primitive bird, archoeopteryx utilized both its fingers and feet. This bird is regarded as one of the missing links in the evolution of birds from reptiles, hence it is called the reptilian bird by some. Another threatened species is the Oil Bird. This occurs in remote caves. The way it orients in pitch darkness makes it peculiar and interesting. The Red-breasted Marshbird is another whose continued existence in Guyana is endangered by chemical spray. The Crowned

Crane and Yellow Crowned Night Heron are also threatened with extinction.

Mammalian Fauna

Mammals are very well represented in Guyana. The opossum, a member of the Marsupialia, referred to by some as a "living fossil," and producing young described as "living abortions," occurs in the country. Five species are recorded here: Common Opossum, also called Yawarri by Guyanese (*Didelphis marsupialis*); Mouse opossum (*Marmosa murina*); Wooly Opossum (*Caluromys philander*); Water Opossum (*Chironectes minimus*) and "Four-eyed" Opossum (*Metachirus nudicaudatus*).

The primates are represented by several species of monkeys. Most of the New World monkeys differ from the Old World types by possessing prehensile tails serving as "fifth hands." They are capable of hanging by their tails and hurling themselves for considerable distances in the forest. They even leap from tree top to tree top like the man on a flying trapeze. The characteristic roar of the beautiful Howler Monkey (*Alouatta seniculus*) can be heard a long distance away. The Squirrel Monkeys (*Saimiri sciureus*) are noted for their gregarious habits. They move in large groups among the bushes of the coastal area. They thrive well in captivity while the Howler Monkeys do so poorly. The White-faced Saki (*Pithecia pithecia*) is found in the forested river banks of the interior. The contrast between the male's white mask and the female's pale yellowish facial stripes facilitates sexual identity in this species. Other species found in Guyana include Bearded Saki (*Chiropotes satanas*), four species of capuchin monkeys (*Cebus capucinus, C. appella, C. nigrivittatus* and *C. albefrons*), Spider Monkey (*Ateles geoffroyi*) and Red-handed tamarin (*Saquinus midas = Tamarin midas*).

Most of these species are reared in captivity, some are eaten (especially the tamarins considered to be palatable) and some, like the sakis, are hunted for their skins which are used as ornaments.

Bats, members of the order Chrioptera and objects of many superstitious stories, are among the mammals found in Guyana. Several species of these nocturnal flying mammals are known to occur in old houses, caves and hollow trees. Those found in Guyana include the fruit-eating, the insectivorous, the carnivorous and the blood-sucking group. *Desmodus rufus*, a true vampire bat, is among the species prevalent in the country.

The edentates in Guyana are the Two-toed and Three-toed Sloths (*Choloepus didactylus* and *Bradypus tridactylus*), the Giant and Silky Anteaters (*Myrmecophaga tridactyla* and *Cyclopes didactylus*), Tamandua or Collared Anteater (*Tamandua tetradactyla*) and the armadillos, namely, the Giant Armadillo (*Priodontes giganteus*), the Naked-Tailed Armadillo (*Cabassous unicinctus*) and the Nine-banded Armadillo (*Dasypus novemcinctus*). The edentates are largely peculiar to Guyana and the rest of South America. They are survivors of ancient Fauna. The species like armadillos found in North America are believed to represent immigrants from the south. Although the name Endentata means "without teeth," the anteaters are the only living form without teeth in the true sense of the word. The sloths, peculiar animals that move and hang from tree limbs in an inverted position, are found in the damp forests and are mainly active at night. The armadillos, with their exotic armor-like covering, are scavengers who live in burrows. Although they usually inhabit savannah areas, they also occur in the forests. The sloths, large anteaters and armadillos are hunted. The Giant Armadillo is now considered scarce in Guyana.

The rodents are well represented. Some of them are favorite game animals. Among the species found here are the prehensile-tailed and hairy procupines (*Coendou prehensilis* and *Sphiggurus melanurus*), the common squirrel (*Sciurus aestuans*), Capybara (*Hydrochoerus hydrochaeris*) the largest existing rodent, Agouti or "Accouri" (*Dasyprocta aquti*) and White-faced Spiny Rat (*Echimys chrysurus*).

A variety of carnivores occur in Guyana. The Tigar Cat (*Felis tigrina*), Puma (*F. concolor*), Ocelot (*F. pardalis*) Jaguarundi (*F. yagouroundi*) and Jaguar (*Panthera onca*) molest domestic animals. Other prevalent carnivorous animals include the Raccoon or "Crab-dog" (*Procyon Cancrivorus*) Kinkajou (*Potos flavus*), Guyana Fox (*Canis cancrivorus savannarum*), Bush dog (*Speothos venaticus*), Coatimundi (*Nasua nasua*), Tayra (*Tayra barbara*) Grison (*Grison vittatus*), Little Otter (*Lutra enuris*), Giant Otter or "Water dog" (*Pteronura brasilensis*), and Margay (*Felis wiedii vigens*). The Giant Otter is one of the species believed to be at the verge of extinction because of hunting pressure. Populations of all species of large cats are in danger throughout the world and, although specific information is lacking, this is probably the case in Guyana.

The Manatee or Sea cow (Sirenia: *Trichechus manatus*), which occurs in marine bays and sluggish rivers, usually in turbid water, is among the Fauna of Guyana. Because of the excellent and fine quality of its meat, hide and oil, this species has been trapped extensively and as a result, its number has greatly diminished. According to Walker *et al, Mammals of this World* (1968), manatees are sometimes used in Guyana to clear canals and other waterways of weed and algae.[4]

The Tapir or Bush cow (Perissodactyla: *Tapirus terrestris*), and some members of the Artiodactyla, which include the collared and white-lipped peccaries (*Tayassu tajacu* and *T. pecari*), the Savannah Deer (*Odocoileus gymnotis*) Red and Gray Brocket (*Mazama americana*, and *M. nemorivaga*), occur in Guyana and are favorite game animals.

Pollution

Today, the desire to preserve a habitable environment for future generations is gaining momentum among scientists, politicians and lay men alike:

There is arising a crisis of world-wide proportions involving developed and developing countries alike—the crisis of the human environment. Portents of this crisis have long been apparent-in the explosive growth of human populations, in the poor integration of a powerful and efficient technology with environmental requirements, in the deterioration of agricultural lands, in the unplanned extension of urban areas, in the decrease of available space and the growing danger of extinction of many forms of animal and plant life. It is becoming apparent that if current trends continue, the future of life on earth could be endangered. It is urgent, therefore, to focus world attention on those problems which threaten humanity in an environment that permits the realization of the

4. E.P. Walker, et al., *Mammals of the World,* 2nd ed., (Baltimore: Johns Hopkins Press, 1968), 1:644.

highest human aspirations, and on the action necessary to deal with them.[5]

Guyana did not remain aloof nor unmindful in the face of growing concern about the pollution problem in many parts of the world. It had and, no doubt, still has, its own share of those problems.

Chemicals and Pesticides

The development and use of pesticides and agricultural chemicals, such as fertilizers, have brought in their wake increased agricultural productivity, greater variety of foodstuffs, and preservatives for their storage. Developing countries like Guyana that have adopted those improvements for an advanced mode of agriculture, feel convinced that they have gained much. As with many things in life, advances in agricultural techniques and pest control usually involve some element of risk.

The Government of Guyana has become aware of the detrimental effects of chemicals and pesticides and has conducted limited analyses of foodstuffs for traces of them. Results of such limited analyses have not given cause for alarm. There is, however, concern about the storing and transportation of pesticides and agricultural products with foodstuffs. There have been reported cases of flour having been imported into the country and stacked close to pesticides, thus becoming contaminated and later found to be the cause of poisoning of people who ate bread baked with that flour. There have been cases where paddy, treated with fungicides and intended for seed and not for food, was mistakenly fed to livestock, thus producing undesireable effects on them.

This fact was succinctly stated by an official of an industrial concern in Puerto Rico: "To live on the earth, we must change our environment. We must cut to build, clear to farm, dig to develop. And for every action upon our environment, there is a possible reaction. Where there is fire, there may be smoke; where there is

5. United Nations Economic and Social Council, *Report of the Secretary-General*, 47th Session (1969), p. 00.

cultivation, there may be erosion; where there is technological wealth, there may be technological waste."

In addition, there have been sporadic reports on the effects of pesticides in use in Guyana on plants, animals and man. Some dogs and cats are known to have died after eating rats killed with rat pellets (poison for killing and controlling rats) and some cattle have died as a result of eating the pellets. After applying "agrocide and lime-stone" in a cane field in September of 1967, several female employees felt ill and first aid treatment was administered to them. Later they were sent to the sugar estate's dispensary for further treatment. In October of the same year the Ministry of Labor and Social Security received letters from Worker's representatives demanding the permanent discontinuation of pesticide spraying operations throughout the country when some of the farmers' crops were destroyed, a considerable number of animals died, and numerous workers became ill. In response, the Ministries of Labor and Social Security, Health, and Agriculture and Natural Resources asked for an investigation of water fodder and soil samples and an examination of the stomachs of dead animals. That study revealed the presence of some traces of poisonous chlorinated hydrocarbon in the samples examined.[6]

Some people have complained of and decried the aerial (or air-craft) and field machinery application of agricultural chemicals and pesticides. The drift of these to other crops, pasture or livestock resulting in their contamination or pollution were reported. Most complaints were made after the use of some of the growth regulator herbicides which, in very low concentrations, are toxic to certain crops. There have been reported cases of harm done to trespassers who unknowingly cut grass, previously treated or contaminated with pesticide, to feed their animals. Also there were cases of harm to animals such as cattle, sheep and donkeys that have grazed on treated crops. Pollution by agricultural chemicals and pesticides is or has been a problem in Guyana. Although the substantiated number of poisoning incidents caused by the use of pesticides, veterinary or agricultural products is relatively minimal, there is a potential hazard in their use.

6. Guyana Government Document, 1968, mimeographed, 14 pp. & Appendices, 8 pp.

Water Pollution

Water pollution is apparently a problem in Guyana. A concerned citizen who preferred to remain anonymous once wrote: "How strange it is that the River Demerara which is so vital to the residents along its banks should be so thoughtlessly used that its value is deteriorating into insignificance! Where have all the fishes gone? This is the question often asked by fishermen who used to boast of big catches. The truth is that the river has become an unhappy place for the fishes to reproduce and thrive. The water is not the same as it used to be." Some people feel that the river has become everybody's rubbish bin. Swimming in it used to be a popular, pleasurable recreation, but it is now much dreaded. Some parents, aware of its pollution or deteriorating condition, dissuade their youngsters from swimming or wading in it. Some residents of the river area claim that the water is very often muddy and discolored. Coats of oil and other tarry substances that contribute to water pollution are frequently seen in the water and on the beaches. Some residents of Christianburg reported that large quantities of fishes are occasionally seen floating dead or struggling for life in the river.

Mining operations in the country are often singled out as a possible source of water pollution, especially in the Linden area where bauxite mining is carried out. Caustic soda, used as an important ingredient in the alumina process, on those occasions when the effluent being thrown away as waste, inadvertently finds its way into creeks and, therefore, into the Demerara River. There occurs immediately or within a short period, what is called a "fish kill"— dead fish are seen floating on the water. This means that the livelihood of a number of people in the river areas is affected. As soon as a complaint is made, however, to the District Commissioner or to the manager of the Alumina Plant, steps are taken to remedy this and to remove the pollution element in the water.

Another source of water pollution emanates from the transfer of oil from the barges to the docks for use in the kilns. The aforementioned officer cited one case where the control tank was left on after the vessels on shore had been filled, and the oil overflowed and found its way into the river. Some captians of ships that go to Port Mackenzie have been charged with contributing to water pollution, accused of discharging their wastes, mostly oil, into the river. Boats and landing places are fouled by such oil, drinking water taken from the river by residents becomes contaminated, and the bark of trees wear an oily film for some time. Some car service stations are also accused of pouring waste oil from vehicles directly into the river. It is further alleged that some people pour human feces into the river, thereby adding to the pollution.

Air Pollution

Air pollution is not an acute problem in Guyana but it does exist on a limited scale. One possible source is particulates (dust) from drying kilns used to reduce the water content of bauxite before shipment to Canada. Industries are rapidly springing up in the country. Light manufacturing industries (producing such products as garments, paints, drinks, soap, canned foods, and animal feed) and flour mills are in operation. A large scale woodpulp and paper industry is about to start. Those are potential sources of industrial wastes and air pollution. They may have contributed to the emission of some air pollutants such as carbon monoxide, sulfur dioxide, oxides of nitrogen and some hydrocarbons in the areas of their operation, especially in Georgetown, where most industrial plants are located. Sulfur dioxide emission caused largely by high sulfur content petroleum in power plants and from industrial production is existent by apparently not at a level to cause alarm.

In Puerto Rico (San Juan) and the continental United States, the primary cause of carbon monoxide pollution is motor vehicles. According to 1970 data, 83% of CO pollution in San Juan and 63.8% in the United States are from that source.[7] Cars are less numerous in Guyana; therefore CO pollution does not pose much problem. If it does, it may be in the cities of Georgetown and New Amsterdam.

7. Osvaldo Ramos, former head of Chemistry Department, University of Puerto Rico. Quoted in *San Juan Star*, November 7, 1970. And *NAPCA Publications*, AP-73, August, 1970.

However, with the increase of industry which may occur in the future because of incentives given by the government (such as an income tax holiday for 5 years to large industries) and increased importation of cars into the country, air pollution is expected to increase and possibly reach a critical level.

Man's pollution of his environment and interference with natural order (referred to as eco-catastrophe or environmental deterioration by some) are now drastically affecting his physical and emotional health. Although pollution is considered a global problem, it is not equally acute in all parts of the world. It is more pronounced in the highly industrialized countries, especially their cities. Guyana remains one of the countries of the world with no acute pollution problem but it has the potential of developing one in the future if no serious preventive measures are taken by the government and the people. Continued efforts to control industrial wastes and other pollutants cannot be overemphasized especially for countries like Guyana where prevention is more relevant now than cure.

Some Recommendations

It is advisable for the Government of Guyana to launch a strong and effective wildlife conservation program. For the preservation of wild animals, especially the rare and threatened species, more game parks and refuges like Kaieteur National Park need to be constructed. In registering his concern about Guyana wildlife and a dire need for its preservation, Mr. Mahamad Hanif, the former Director of Guyana Museum and Zoo and the editor of its journal, quoted this excerpt* from the *Journal of the Fauna Preservation Society:*

No resident mammal or bird of British Guiana is known to have become extinct during 2,000 years. This had been due to the extensive forests and small human populations of the past, but these factors cannot be relied upon indefinitely. The time to preserve animals and plants is before the threat to their existence has developed strongly.[8]

* Quotation attributed to "Oryx" (full name not given). (Ed.)

8. *Journal of the Fauna Preservation Society*, quoted by Mahamad Hanif, in "Wildlife Preservation?" *Journal of Guyana Museum and Zoo*, 42 (1966):57.

After commenting on the heavily forested mountains, the great savannahs of the southwest, the innumerable rivers that criss-cross the landscape and the amazing wildlife that these support, he said:

> Within recent years, however, the teeming wildlife has been subjected to vicious indiscriminate slaughter. Arapaima, Caiman, Capybara, Otter and Turtle, have been over-hunted and face extinction if the massacre goes on unchecked.[9]

Mr. Hanif's note of warning needs to be heeded.

The plan by the Demerara Bauxite Co., Ltd. to control dust from bauxite plants in Makenzie by installing electrostatic dust collectors is commendable. It is hoped that with the recent nationalization of that firm this plan will not be abandoned. Similar effective measures should be taken to discontinue or minimize the pollution of the navigable Demerara River. The reported practice of the Demerara Bauxite Company in applying remedial measures only when people complain about pollution and some fish have already been killed, is a panacea that leaves much to be desired and may be doing more harm than good.

Something must be done to preserve the indigenous and migratory birds that winter in the country. The already existing Wild Birds Protection Ordinance should be enforced by the government.

Efforts should be made to eliminate excessive hunting and indiscriminate killing of animals for food, ornamentation or pecuniary purposes.

The University of Guyana should play a definite role in the formulation of a scientific basis for conservation. Ecological studies should be emphasized, especially among the life sciences faculty. Incentives to conduct investigation in environmental biology should be given to qualified faculty through government research grants. A research institute migh also be founded to concentrate on environmental or ecological studies. As it was lucidly put by Mr. David Dominick of The U. S. Environmental Protection Agency:

> It is the scientists, engineers and technicians, perhaps more than any of the other professions or disciplines who can contribute the most to a rational effective program of resource management. They will provide solutions to the awesome and complex

environmental problem in the decades immediately ahead. They must, however, enjoy the total cooperation of government and avenues of communication must be clear at all times to permit full discussion and consultation.[9]

It is advisable to create an Environmental Quality Board where industry, government and the public can talk over environmental problems, obtain guidance and formulate action. Government should provide the standards and regulations that industries will follow. Government should demarcate those areas wherein the environment must be improved and other areas wherein it must be maintained. For prospective industries wanting to locate in Guyana, strict industrial zoning should be established to assign industries to areas favorable for pollution control.

The Guyanese government might look into the possibility of adopting some of the measures used by the United States to abate ambient degradation such as:

1. Clean Air Amendments of 1970, considered the best plan for clean air that the United States has ever had;*
2. The Refuse Act of 1899, which prohibits dumping of un- authorized materials into navigable waters of the United States without a permit. Industries are required to obtain discharge permits;
3. The 1970 Water Quality Improvement Act, which introduced the requirement that local government certify that their water quality standards will not be violated by a new installation.

Corporate or industrial policy should relate to government action by closely reflecting what the Government of Guyana wants in air and water quality and solid waste control. The policy should show awareness of Guyana's unique environment and indicate that the responsibility of protecting it is just as great, if not greater, than in other areas of the world. Companies should make this policy known to their employees and charge them with a share of the responsibility for contributing to the plant or facilities' objective by exercising due

9. Quoted by Chad J. Barbone, Puerto Rico Sun Oil Co., in a talk during the Industrial Pollution Seminar, San Juan, Puerto Rico, May 20, 1971.

* The key to these is to provide local jurisdiction with rules and guidelines to establish and maintain acceptable air quality standards.

care and precaution to control and prevent air and water pollution in the performance of their duties.

The petrochemical industry and/or agro-industry, eager to sell pesticides, fertilizers, and farm machinery in Guyana, should employ a corporate policy which is in the interest of the nation and not only for its own profit.

Industry must adopt the policy of frank disclosure to the proper agencies of what their problems are in meeting regulations and how solutions are to be implemented. It should help the government to understand the problems of industrialization and pollution control so that realistic industrial promotion can go forth and continue to create jobs. *(See Addendum, pp. 82-85)*

ADDENDUM, *Wildlife and Pollution*

Global hue and cry about pollution

The outcry about pollution has reached every nook and corner of the world with the result that urban areas and country sides, developed and underdeveloped countries of the world show a great concern.

Environmental studies are booming and books, monographs and articles on them are being produced in large numbers.

The ecologists talk about pollution in our ecosystem and stress the fact that man should, and must, learn to live in dynamic equilibrium within the ecosystem, rather than seek dominion over it and destruction of it. They strongly warn that man's heedless outpouring of noxious wastes is overwhelming the biosphere's ability to cleanse itself. The American Association for the Advancement of Science devoted 40 symposia at its annual meeting to environmental dangers. The news media issue almost daily reports on assorted ecological disasters—oil spills, fish kills and nuclear radiation. The Pentagon was forced to discontinue the use of Agent Orange (2,4,5,-T), a herbicide, as a chemical defoliant in Viet Nam as biologists who returned from there argued that defoliation, meant merely to denude trees that have provided cover for the enemy, was doing incalculable long-term damage to food crops, the soil and the people themselves. A Harris poll taken in 1970 showed that Americans regard pollution as "the most serious" problem confronting their community— well ahead of crime, drugs and poor schools. In the summer of 1970 the dangers of polluted air were dramatized by the smog that blanketed most of Eastern Seabord for days especially New York City. After a nationwide sampling, the Bureau of Water Hygiene reported that 5% of the water was contaminated and 11% was smelly, discolored or foul. It was reported that dead fish clogged the surface of brackish Florida Escambia Bay. State and country officials blamed the kill on industrial discharge from three companies.[1] In the spring of 1970 dangerous concentrations of mercury were found in fish from the great Lakes region. It was also reported in tuna, swordfish and Arctic seals. It became apparent that this industrial waste had tainted the oceans to an intolerable extent. After sailing across the Atlantic in a reed boat in the summer of 1970 explorer Thor Heyerdahl reported that stinking nodules of oil covered a 1,400-mile stretch of mid-ocean. Apparently the oil was dumped by ships cleaning their tanks.

Many other countries besides America have become aware of and have showed concern about pollution problems. Russia, Sweden and New Zealand banned the use of DDT. After 48 school children were felled by photochemical smog in Tokyo in the summer of 1970, environmental disruption became Japan's top issue. Italy was reported to be suffering from traffic congestion and choking with solid waste; 4,320 of its 5,000 mile coastline, were said to be polluted by municipal and industrial wastes. West German's Lake Constance, the country's biggest source of fresh water was reported to have turned reddish-brown because of contamination and said to be going the way of "dead" lake Erie. Red China which is becoming rapidly industrialized admitted that its cities were also beset with environmental problems. In the continent of Africa, a newspaper headline said: "Polution Threatens Africa's Wildlife" with convulsions. It is believed that mercury poisoning produces fatigue and irritability in the early stages, and perhaps many years later, numbness of the limbs, tremors, blurred vision, mental derangement and even death.

DDT belongs to a category of chemicals called chlorinated hydrocarbons. Once introduced into the food web, chlorinated hydrocarbons are also able to move up from phytoplankton to zooplankton, to fish, and sometimes to birds or mammals. They may also move up a terrestrial food web, starting with insects. They become more and more concentrated as they are retained by animals of higher trophic levels. For instance, some elm trees in the midwest of the U.S. were sprayed heavily to control the bark beetle, vector of Dutch elm disease. Earthworms capable of tolerating fairly large doses of DDT picked up the insecticide from the soil and stored it in their body tissues. Robins arriving in the spring ate the earthworms and died.

1. The *Times-Picayune*, New Orleans, La., Sept. 4, 1970.

82

DDT residues in the eggs of fish can affect the hatching success and survival of young fish. In Jasper National Park, Canada, there was 70% mortality of brook trout fry hatched from eggs with 0.46 ppm of DDT residues. In Michigan, 700,000 coho salmon fry died in hatcheries in 1968. They were hatched from eggs with DDT residues of 1.5% to 3 ppm. The DDT concentration is in the oil globule in the yolk and when the yolk in consumed, the poison kills by attacking the nervous system. In 1968, it was discovered that DDT slows down photosynthesis in marine plant life.

Some chemical pollutants are carcinogenic and some affect the unborn baby. They are absorbed by the mother, go through the placental barrier and are passed on to the child before birth. Some of these feticides are DDT, epoxides and mechlycines.

Detergents containing phosphates cause blooms of algae which rapidly deplete the O_2 supply. The algae and aquatic animals then die. This process is called entrophication.

Insecticides such as DDT used for spraying agricultural crops have been found in varying percentages in the liver and lungs of cattle and human beings. Evidence that pesticides have long-term lethal effect on human beings has been accumulating.

"The simple act of introducing material into the air is not air pollution. If the materials produce or contribute to an adverse effect on the health and well-being of men or interfere with his normal and reasonable activities or use of property, it is air pollution."[3]

Knowledge about air pollution is probably age-old. Primitive man must have detected air pollution in the form of smoke when he moved his fire into his cave. Air pollution, to many, means smoke, but there is more to it than this. Smoke has been, however, and still is an important aspect of pollution. As far back as the 13th century, smoke in London was considered so obnoxious that regulations were imposed on the use of coal.

Particulates

Particulate pollutants are finely divided solids or liquid droplets. Their sources are heavy industries, automobiles, power stations, large steel plants, and backyard incinerators. The larger particles fall back close to the source, depending on the wind, and become dirt. The finer particles travel far. They are capable of being buoyed up by the slightest air movement. They hardly settle out and are referred to as aerosol. They diffuse into the air like gas finally becoming diluted or hydrolized in the presence of moisture to give acidic or basic reactions. They are the dirt and grime that seep into buildings, soil clothes, reduce visibility and possibly affect human health. They are incriminated as possible causes of irritation of the respiratory passages. They and such materials in the air cause accelerated weathering and corrosion of all exposed materials and add to the cost of up-keep and maintenance of property.

Sulfur Dioxide (SO_2)

Sulfur dioxide, produced mainly by burning of fossil fuels (oil and coal), and wood and charcoal react with water or moisture to give sulfuric acid (H_2SO_4) which enters plants through the stomata and causes destruction of the mesophyl and scotching of the margins of leaves giving them brown or dark color.

An evidence of what SO_2 can do to vegetation is seen from the swelter at Ducktown, Tennessee where a "little desert" still remains after almost 50 years. It causes faster deterioration of materials. Cleopatra's Needle, a stone sculpture donated to New York City by Egypt in 1920, has been partly deteriorated as a result of SO_2, a problem in that city.

With respect to human health, SO_2 plus water (H_2SO_4) and some other air pollutants are believed to cause chronic bronchitis, pulmonary emphysema, lung cancer and other or varied respiratory diseases.

Carbon monoxide (CO)

Carbon monoxide (CO), produced by motor vehicles' fuel combustion, industrial processes and solid waste disposals causes chlorosis on leaves of some plants. It causes

2. Stanley A. Hall, "The Place of Insecticides," *Yearbook of Agriculture: Farmer's World* (Washington: U.S. Government Printing Office, 1964), pp. 113-117.

3. C.S. Brandt, "Air is for More Than Breathing," *Yearbook of Agriculture: A Place to Live* (Washington: U.S. Government Printing Office, 1963) pp. 121-132.

asphyxia, a lack of oxygen or excess of carbon dioxide in the body resulting from interruption of breathing, and sometimes causes unconsciousness. It displaces oxygen from hemoglobin to form carboxyhemoglobin.

Carbon dioxide (CO_2)

Excess inhalation of this gas, produced by increased use of fossil fuels, also causes asphyxia. CO_2 content in the air is believed to be increasing. According to Dr. C.D. Leake, former president of American Association for the Advancement of Science, since this chemical is important in the heat balance of the earth, such an increase is of great concern. Excessive CO_2 in the earth's atmosphere could cause climatic warming which might result in the melting of polar ice and flooding of our coasts.

Oxides of Nitrogen (NO_x)

These are produced mainly as a result of fuel combustion. They can contribute to corrosion and material deterioration under certain conditions. With ultra violet light from the sun, they are converted to organic nitrogen compounds such as: 1) peroxyacetyl nitrate (PAN) which is an eye irritant and causes conjunctivitis (also believed to cause lung cancer, emphysema, and heart aliments); 2) peroxybuyl nitrate; and 3) peroxypropionil nitrate.

Ozone (O_3)

Ozone is produced by oxidation of nitrogen oxide. It causes emphysema in human beings, and, possibly cancer of the lung. It also causes scorching of leaves. The leaves are bleached white or creamy white by it.

Smog

Smog is a term coined in England from "smoke" and "fog" and describes the air pollution situation in London. Smog is basically a smoke problem of heavy particulate matter and SO_2 complicated and worsened by fog. The term is used in America to describe air pollution in Los Angeles and several other large metropolitan areas.

Unsaturated hydrocarbons such as methylene, acetylene, and propylene, resulting from handling fuel and from unburned fuel from auto exhaust, boilers, etc. are generally gaseous and are components of smog. In high concentrations they cause undesirable effects including odor problems and they undergo photo-oxidation to produce compounds that are irritating to mucous membranes. Under poor weather conditions that impede diffusion or large-scale dilution but permits exposure to sunlight, these hydrocarbons plus nitrogen oxides result in a smog of the Los Angeles variety.[4] Such air pollution condition is now generally referred to as photochemical smog to distinguish it from the smoke-fog type. The term also implies that the condition results from reactions between pollutants induced by light. Aerosols and O_3 are believed to be formed from such reactions. PAN is believed to be just one member of a class of compounds of similar nature and effect that can be produced by photochemical smog.

Smog is a big air pollution problem that causes considerable injury to plants. Its effect have caused rather severe economic losses to vegetable crops in the Los Angeles area. Apart from reduced visibility and eye irritation, lesions on plant leaves are characteristic of photochemical smog.

Arsenic and Fluoride

Some of the adverse effects of air pollution on animals can be attributed to two toxicants, arsenic and flouride.

Arsenic problems arise as a result of smelter operations. Arsenic is a common trace

4. Brandt, *ibid.*

element of many sulfide ores. In the process of heating to drive off the sulfur, arsenic is volatilized. It condenses again and settles on vegetation. Cattle grazing on the vegetation could become poisoned.

Fluorides are produced by utilization of fluorate in some industries like glass manufacture, cement, phosphate fertilizers and by aluminum refineries. Areas with high levels of atmospheric fluorides may adversely affect both plants and animals. Gaseous fluorides cause injury to plants depending on the amount absorbed. They cause discoloration near the tip of plant leaves and characteristic leaf lesions. When livestock feeds on vegetation containing such fluorides, they suffer from fluorosis, characterized by swelling of the joints, and they eventually die.

General

In many areas the automobile represents a major source of organic materials vented into the atmosphere. This means that the output of organic compounds from automobiles is greatest where the traffic is greatest thus compounding the problem of pollution. Automobile emissions of nitrogen oxides and hydrocarbons must be abated.

Water pollution is the presence in water of any substance that impairs any of its legitimate uses. The legitimate uses include "water for public water supplies, recreation, agriculture and industry, the preservation of fish and wildlife and esthetic purposes."[5]

The extent of pollution in a body of water can be measured in part by the amount of organic waste in it.

Many organic wastes can be degraded by biochemical means, either in a naturally free-flowing stream or in an artificially created industrial waste treatment plant. But some pollutants cannot be similarly degraded or easily removed. Among these are minerals and acids from mining and industrial activities, substances like pesticides, detergents, and petro-chemical wastes.

Knowledge about controls to eliminate pollution remains deficient. However, enough is known to reduce many pollutants. Genuine efforts should therefore be made to reduce them in all countries.

5. J.J. Flannery, "Water Polution: A Public Concern," *Yearbook of Agriculture: A Place to Live* (Washington: U.S. Government Printing Office, 1963), pp. 116-120.

CONTRIBUTORS

ALEXANDER D. ACHOLONU was born in Owerri, Nigeria and was a Nigeria Government Scholar. He was Professor and Chairman of the Department of Biology at Inter American University, Hato Rey Campus. He holds a Ph.D. degree in Zoology from Colorado State University. Dr. Acholonu has published over 25 scientific and non-scientific papers.

VED P. DUGGAL is Associate Professor, Department of Economics and Business Administration at Inter American University of Puerto Rico, San Germán Campus. He received his B.A. from Punjab University, his M.A. from Delhi University, and his Ph.D. from the Netherlands School of Economics. He has taught at the University of Glasgow, Scotland; Middle East Technical University, Turkey; and University of Windsor, Canada.

BRIAN IRVING is presently Dean of Academic Affairs, Academic Programs at Military Bases, Inter American University. He is a past Director of the Caribbean Institute and Study Center for Latin America (CISCLA), which sponsored the Guyana study. He was also Chairman of History and Political Science at Inter American University. Mr. Irving holds a B.A. from U.C.L.A. and an M.A. from Wesleyan. He is presently concluding his doctoral studies.

YERETH KNOWLES is Associate Professor in the Political Science Department at Inter American University, San Germán. She holds a B.A. and an M.A. from the University of Wisconsin and has passed her Ph.D. examination at the Institute of International Relations, Geneva. She is presently engaged in writing *History of Regional Cooperation in the Caribbean.*

HAROLD A. LUTCHMAN is Guyanese, and a member of the staff of the Department of Government and Public Administration of the University of Guyana. He holds degrees from the University of the West Indies and Manchester University. During the twenty-fifth anniversary session of the United Nations, Dr. Lutchman was a member of the Guyana Delegation. He is the author of a number of articles concerning the politics of Guyana.

DELLA WALKER is Associate Professor of Sociology and Anthropology at Inter American University in San Germán. She received her M.A. from Washington State University. She has traveled extensively throughout the Caribbean and is presently working on a project with Dr. Charles Fugler of Oklahoma City University, observing the effects of civilization on Amerindians in the interior of Guyana.

BRIAN WEARING is a Professor of History at the University of Canterbury in Christchurch, New Zealand. An expert in Russian language and Cryptography, he is a graduate of Oxford University where he specialized in the history of the United States and Latin America. He was visiting exchange professor at Inter American University in San Germán at the time of the CISCLA Guyana study.

Institute of Commonwealth Studies
Oxford